Number 110
Summer 2006

New Directions for Evaluation

Jean A. King
Editor-in-Chief

Pitfalls and Pratfalls:
Null and Negative Findings
in Evaluating Interventions

Cynthia Hudley
Robert Nash Parker
Editors

PITFALLS AND PRATFALLS: NULL AND NEGATIVE FINDINGS
IN EVALUATING INTERVENTIONS
Cynthia Hudley, Robert Nash Parker (eds.)
New Directions for Evaluation, no. 110
Jean A. King, Editor-in-Chief

Gift 8|07

H
6 2
,P574
2006

Microfilm copies of issues and articles are available in 16mm and 35mm,
as well as microfiche in 105mm, through University Microfilms Inc., 300
North Zeeb Road, Ann Arbor, Michigan 48106-1346.

New Directions for Evaluation is indexed in Contents Pages in Education,
Higher Education Abstracts, and Sociological Abstracts.

NEW DIRECTIONS FOR EVALUATION (ISSN 1097-6736, electronic ISSN
1534-875X) is part of The Jossey-Bass Education Series and is published
quarterly by Wiley Subscription Services, Inc., A Wiley Company, at
Jossey-Bass, 989 Market Street, San Francisco, California 94103-1741.

SUBSCRIPTIONS cost $100.00 for U.S./Canada/Mexico; $124 international.
For institutions, agencies, and libraries, $185 U.S.; $225 Canada; $259
international. Prices subject to change.

EDITORIAL CORRESPONDENCE should be addressed to the Editor-in-Chief,
Jean A. King, University of Minnesota, 330 Wulling Hall, 86 Pleasant
Street SE, Minneapolis, MN 55455.

www.josseybass.com

Editorial Policy and Procedures

New Directions for Evaluation, a quarterly sourcebook, is an official publication of the American Evaluation Association. The journal publishes empirical, methodological, and theoretical works on all aspects of evaluation. A reflective approach to evaluation is an essential strand to be woven through every volume. The editors encourage volumes that have one of three foci: (1) craft volumes that present approaches, methods, or techniques that can be applied in evaluation practice, such as the use of templates, case studies, or survey research; (2) professional issue volumes that present issues of import for the field of evaluation, such as utilization of evaluation or locus of evaluation capacity; (3) societal issue volumes that draw out the implications of intellectual, social, or cultural developments for the field of evaluation, such as the women's movement, communitarianism, or multiculturalism. A wide range of substantive domains is appropriate for *New Directions for Evaluation;* however, the domains must be of interest to a large audience within the field of evaluation. We encourage a diversity of perspectives and experiences within each volume, as well as creative bridges between evaluation and other sectors of our collective lives.

The editors do not consider or publish unsolicited single manuscripts. Each issue of the journal is devoted to a single topic, with contributions solicited, organized, reviewed, and edited by a guest editor. Issues may take any of several forms, such as a series of related chapters, a debate, or a long article followed by brief critical commentaries. In all cases, the proposals must follow a specific format, which can be obtained from the editor-in-chief. These proposals are sent to members of the editorial board and to relevant substantive experts for peer review. The process may result in acceptance, a recommendation to revise and resubmit, or rejection. However, the editors are committed to working constructively with potential guest editors to help them develop acceptable proposals.

Jean A. King, Editor-in-Chief
University of Minnesota
330 Wulling Hall
86 Pleasant Street SE
Minneapolis, MN 55455
e-mail: kingx004@umn.edu

CONTENTS

EDITORS' NOTES

Evaluation research, like most other scientific fields of inquiry, has a bias toward "successful" outcomes. Findings, whether they are qualitative, quantitative, or some combination of both types of data, are typically celebrated when it is demonstrated that at least some if not all of the effects of a treatment or intervention were anticipated by those who developed and implemented the program. However, every advanced graduate student has already heard about or experienced the dreaded problem of null findings or "What do I do now that my intervention or treatment has had zero discernable effects?" A negative effect or a case in which the treatment or intervention appears to disadvantage the study group compared to a comparison or control group can be even more devastating to evaluators, to program designers, and potentially to participants. As well, it is no small consequence that the ability to publish null or negative evaluation research findings is well known to be almost nonexistent. Therefore, most evaluation research practitioners have more than one report stuck in their files, never to see the light of day, because despite their best efforts, the analysis showed no or, even worse, negative impacts on the participants' outcomes.

Yet a true commitment to the advancement of knowledge and, in evaluation research, the advancement of practice and evidence-driven social policy demands that negative and null findings be shared with future evaluators, program designers, and potential intervention participants alike. If we remain ignorant of past errors in dysfunctional or ineffective programs or misdirected evaluation strategies, are we not doomed to repeat those errors in yet-to-be-conceived and developed programs and evaluations? We believe that the unfortunate cycle of history repeating itself must not be the inevitable destiny of evaluation research.

The purpose of this volume, therefore, is to shed light on null and negative findings, the pitfalls and pratfalls if you will, of evaluation studies. We use interventions designed to reduce or prevent youth violence as examples of evaluation studies that can shed light into the dim corners of past mistakes. Youth violence prevention is a particularly timely topic, given its place at the heart of a current public discussion on the state of American youth that cries out for evidence-based practice and policy decisions. In most cases, knowledge about problems, errors, and mishaps that can help produce negative or null outcomes in an intervention study is the stuff of research seminar comments, hallway discussions, and barroom digressions late in the evening at professional meetings. This volume brings those important lessons into the larger discussion of evaluation and public policy.

NEW DIRECTIONS FOR EVALUATION, no. 110, Summer 2006   © Wiley Periodicals, Inc.
Published online in Wiley InterScience (www.interscience.wiley.com) • DOI: 10.1002/ev.182

The authors of the chapters in this volume are not only admitting to a set of problems and shortcomings but also analyzing these unfortunate outcomes to draw general lessons, cautions, and advice for others following in their footsteps who want to evaluate youth violence prevention efforts—or social and behavioral interventions in general—without repeating these same mistakes. Sometimes the evidence shows that failure in a particular case was due to a fatal flaw in the design of the program or the evaluation study that was all but impossible to see beforehand but is avoidable once you know what to look for. Other chapters document changing circumstances and larger social, political, and economic issues that undermine program or research designs and produce unexpected outcomes. Even circumstances that are beyond the control of the evaluator have implications for the design, implementation, and analysis of future evaluation studies.

Although the chapters presented here focus on youth violence prevention, every evaluator should be interested in these detailed assessments of failures and null findings. Themes common to all evaluations are evident in these examples. Chapter One discusses a problem common to many types of intervention programs designed to effect behavior change. Changes in behavior are typically the consequence of changes in attitude, and programs are not always sufficiently powerful to change attitudes in a manner that contravenes established community norms and folkways, no matter how beneficial the changed behavior might be to the community. Although successful with some objectives, evaluation data demonstrate that the program in this example did not effect a core set of attitudinal and behavioral changes targeted by the intervention—in this example, attitudes toward firearms. If the contexts in which participants live support the attitudes and behaviors targeted for change, interventions at the individual level may inevitably prove ineffective. Changing the local culture may be a difficult but necessary precondition for certain kinds of behavioral interventions to have a chance to be effective.

Chapter Two presents a dilemma common to the evaluation of any program for youth. In many cases, an intervention can be undermined by a refusal of subjects to buy into the program, to reject services offered, or to change their attitudes sufficiently to allow the intervention to occur and its impact to be assessed. Any intervention involving youth must somehow, in the current legal climate, involve parents; many evaluators will read with interest how failures to secure parental participation, permission, or endorsement affected evaluation results. Perhaps more important, these lessons may shed light on how to increase such participation by the design of either the evaluation or the intervention. Dosage is a fundamental issue in evaluation and intervention, and most readers will benefit from the discussion of low-dosage cases and analytical approaches to more appropriately analyze such cases.

Mass media campaigns, a staple of intervention strategies because of their potential reach, are the subject of the lessons presented in Chapter

Three. Many media campaigns fail, and they can be expensive, so most evaluators will appreciate the discussion of measurement problems inherent in the evaluation, missteps in intervention design, and difficulties in implementation that are detailed in this chapter. Particularly when dealing with sensitive topics, participants may not be forthcoming or others may block access to information, especially if participants are children, seriously compromising the measurement of effects. The chapter also presents lessons learned that are unique to the mass media, and the pitfalls inherent in the reach of media beyond the audience who participates in the evaluation. Given the expense of media campaigns, pressure from outside sources more often controls decisions about design and implementation, as every evaluator knows, with potentially troublesome consequences for the evaluation.

Larger societal trends are clearly outside the control of an evaluator and often of a program designer. Chapter Four presents a lesson on the broader social and political forces that can have dramatic effects on the implementation and outcomes of an intervention. There is not much an evaluator can do when the political or economic climate that once supported an intervention experiences a sea change. This chapter describes the complex aftermath of just such a change in the policy climate. Exploring the impact of these larger societal trends can help us better understand the failure of an intervention that is designed to aid exactly those people who are most negatively affected by such downturns in economic and social policy. This discussion will be of special interest to most if not all evaluators, as any intervention can become subject to such forces at any time.

Local contextual effects of all kinds are yet another source of influence on programs and evaluations that can unexpectedly affect outcomes of interest. Chapter Five eloquently details the importance of considering contextual issues very carefully. Regardless of the content, a school-based intervention that relies on classroom teachers for implementation, as was the case in this example, rests on a series of assumptions about the context of the school and its capacity to participate fully in the intervention. These assumptions are crucial to the success of an intervention and must be accounted for in an evaluation design. If only later the evaluator learns that half the classrooms are without teachers on an average day, the context has rather effectively doomed the intervention. All evaluators will be interested in how local context affects the intervention and what an evaluator can do if faced with such a problem.

It has also become standard operating procedure to build in both qualitative and quantitative data collection as part of any evaluation. As evaluators we are all convinced of the wisdom that multiple and coordinated sources of data reveal a much richer sense of the impact of an intervention than either type of data would on its own. Yet what happens if the two sources of data are in direct discord, or if one source of data is of questionable validity? Chapter Six deals with this issue of interest to every evaluator, offers support for well-known effects like observer reactivity, and discusses hard lessons learned about the power of social relationships outside the intervention program to shape the nature of the evaluation. Evaluators of all kinds of programs for children will gain insights into the social dimension of evaluation research and how it can be successfully addressed.

In short, we bravely focus the light of day on our mishaps and misdemeanors, our pitfalls and pratfalls, in the hope that our community of evaluators will see themselves in us and know they are not alone. Our desire is that others should learn lessons from our misfortunes that allow them in the future to do better than we have done in the past. Our collected analyses of how and why we have failed will illuminate larger questions of policy and practice that should serve to improve the design, implementation, support, and evaluation of efforts to prevent youth violence in particular and programs and evaluations of behavior change in general. If this effort results in more effective evaluations and more success in enhancing the behavioral competence of our youth, we are more than justified in going boldly where no researchers have gone before—airing our dirty laundry in public.

ROBERT NASH PARKER *is professor of sociology and director of the Presley Center for Crime and Justice Studies at the University of California, Riverside.*

CYNTHIA HUDLEY *is professor in the Gevirtz Graduate School of Education at the University of California, Santa Barbara, and director of the graduate emphasis in Child and Adolescent Development.*

NEW DIRECTIONS FOR EVALUATION • DOI: 10.1002/ev

1

This chapter, which documents lessons from a collaborative project involving researchers, youth service organizations, and a private grant-making foundation, notes the challenge of changing deeply rooted attitudes and behaviors.

Qualitative Lessons from a Community-Based Violence Prevention Project with Null Findings

Kirk R. Williams, Sabrina Arredondo Mattson

The Youth Handgun Violence Prevention Project (YHVPP) was conducted in the Denver Metropolitan Area from July 1999 to June 2002. Several factors associated with youth attitudes and behaviors regarding handguns were identified and verified empirically (Williams and Arredondo Mattson, 2002). Interventions were designed to modify these factors and to evaluate their effectiveness in changing youth knowledge of the legal consequences of carrying and using handguns, attitudes reflecting excitement and power associated with handguns, and self-reported carrying and use of these weapons.

The evaluation showed that while the YHVPP achieved its general objectives, the effectiveness of the interventions implemented was not empirically demonstrated. The evaluation found no intervention effects indicating an increase in anti-handgun attitudes, knowledge of legal

Note: We want to express our sincere appreciation to the Colorado Trust for launching and providing sole financial support for the Colorado Youth Handgun Violence Prevention Project (Colorado Trust Grant Number 99048), with a special acknowledgment going to Carol Breslau, senior program officer, who participated fully as a contributing partner in the project. The project would not have been possible without the invaluable involvement of several people we would like to thank (in alphabetical order): Jim Bernuth, Michelle Binkowski, Matt Bovenzi, Shay Bright, Mary Ann Fremgen, Elizabeth Loescher, Sherry Powers, Clifton Rogers, and Regan Suhay.

NEW DIRECTIONS FOR EVALUATION, no. 110, Summer 2006 © Wiley Periodicals, Inc.
Published online in Wiley InterScience (www.interscience.wiley.com) • DOI: 10.1002/ev.183

consequences, or a decrease in handgun carrying. Regardless, this research provided important findings on youth's access to handguns. Perceived accessibility to handguns was associated with an increase in pro-handgun attitudes and handgun carrying at post-test. Moreover, perceiving handguns as safely locked was associated with a reduction in the perceived access to these potentially deadly weapons. These empirical relations suggest an important implication for policy: all things being equal, removing handguns from homes could decrease their perceived accessibility, the endorsement of the symbolic power of handguns, and the frequency of handgun carrying. If handguns are not removed from the home, locking them may reduce their perceived accessibility, which in turn might also reduce pro-handgun attitudes and handgun carrying (Williams and Arredondo Mattson, 2003).

A summary of the lessons learned requires discussing the insights of the program staff working directly with the youth, the program officer from the grant-making foundation funding the project, and the researchers. These insights provide a more qualitative window into the project and are important for two reasons. First, they assist in the interpretation of evaluation results. For example, input from the service providers weaves an understanding of why interventions did not have statistically significant effects on designated outcomes. Issues about maintaining the fidelity of the intervention design or administering the intervention can be addressed. In short, if the program results are contrary to expectations, lessons learned from the project team may help to explain why. Second, an important goal was to learn from the experience of building a team of researchers, program providers, and foundation staff working collaboratively to improve programming and research to reduce youth handgun violence. The following insights provide a more in-depth look at some of the challenges of such a collaborative effort. Even though the results of the previous analysis found little evidence of intervention effects, the following insights feature "success stories" not detected by the quantitative evaluation data but potentially useful for improving programs.

The YHVPP project unfolded in three phases. The first phase began with a six-month planning period that provided an opportunity to review the handgun violence and prevention literature. The project team collaboratively crafted the interventions that were infused in services already provided by three youth service agencies and also agreed upon the quasi-experimental evaluation to assess intervention effectiveness. This collaborative planning process included constructing the questionnaire for pre-testing and post-testing participating youth, which was informative although challenging. It was informative in that service providers drew from their experience with youth to ensure that the content and wording of items was compatible with their clientele. It was challenging in that items were dropped to abbreviate the questionnaire, making it suitable for administration in the normal work routines of these agencies and realistic in terms of the attention span and comprehension level of the youth served. Compromises were reached that balanced the responsibilities of the agencies, the nature of their youth, and the research objectives of the evaluation project.

The second phase, during which interventions and data collection protocol were piloted, began January 1, 2000. This phase ended in summer of 2000 and resulted in modifications of all aspects of the project, from the services offered to youth to the questionnaire itself. After needed adjustments were completed, the implementation phase commenced in the fall of 2001. Once the project received full clearances for the protection of human subjects, including a certificate of confidentiality, youth assent and parental consent were obtained. Youth were then pre-tested and post-tested on a rolling basis from that point until December 31, 2002.

Participating youth were drawn from the normal operations of three youth service agencies located in the Denver Metropolitan Area. These agencies provide services primarily in the inner city. Two of the agencies provide counseling and educational, recreational, and life skills training for wellness to their clientele. Youth typically are referred to courts for weapon violations, violent behavior, or other criminal activities. However, some youth are also referred by parents or other adult guardians for similar behavioral problems. These two agencies implemented their interventions in their counseling and life skills training groups (hence, group-based interventions), usually held at their organizational sites. The third agency provides conflict resolution training for children, adolescents, and adults by teaching nonviolent methods for dealing with conflict and anger in schools, organizations, and the larger community. The training emphasizes both individual change and cultural change. For the purposes of the YHVPP, this agency worked in schools, focusing on those in the inner city likely to experience high rates of youth handgun violence.

The insights and lessons learned from this project are grouped into the following topic areas: the characteristics of the youth who seemed to be more receptive to the interventions, aspects of program implementation that seemed to help gain cooperation of the youth, and challenges and accomplishments. Four sources of information were used to capture these insights: exit focus groups, meeting notes, progress reports, and observations from the program officer and the researchers. A facilitator conducted focus groups with the collaborating agencies, including first-line staff working with youth (n = 7), program coordinators (n = 3), project directors (n = 3), the foundation program officer, and researchers (n = 2). The focus groups were tape recorded and then transcribed. The coded transcriptions served as the main source of data for the discussion that follows. The focus group data were augmented with relevant information from the project meetings held monthly during the planning and pilot phases, then bimonthly during the implementation phase. Each meeting began with project updates provided by a representative from each program, the researchers, and the foundation program officer.

Everyone was encouraged to discuss challenges and accomplishments that were puzzling or gratifying. Relevant meeting notes were coded into the four topic areas and incorporated into the lessons learned from the project. The third source of data came from the six-month progress reports. Two sections of the progress reports provided particularly useful information on the lessons learned from the project: (1) the program delivery questions referring to implementation challenges and accomplishments and (2) the narrative section documenting important experiences from the director, staff, and youth in the project. Finally, the foundation program officer and the researchers added other observations for those who might pursue such an endeavor.

Characteristics of Youth

Five characteristics seemed to distinguish youth who were more cooperative during the interventions from those who were not: (1) age, (2) continued enrollment in school, (3) personal experience with the more serious consequences of handgun use, (4) a lack of alternative sanctions in school or the criminal justice system, and (5) parental involvement. With regard to age, younger rather than older program participants seemed to be more open and receptive to the interventions. This was true of high school freshmen among the youth in the school-based program. Program staff suggested that freshmen may be more open-minded and not yet highly influenced by the older youth.

Second, for youth in the community-based programs, those still in school seemed to be more open and receptive than youth who were not. Mixing youth who were still attending school with youth who were out of school made it difficult to engage any of the youth. As one service provider described the matter, "Youth who were not in school were not comfortable with a classroom setting or even group discussions. They were often distracting to the rest of the group." Youth who were not in school were more resistant to change and had behavioral issues such as having a tendency to act out and not listen, making it difficult to have a group discussion or cover the curriculum. In contrast, youth in school were accustomed to a learning environment and were more likely to attend the handgun curriculum classes and participate in the discussions and lessons.

Youth with a lack of alternative sanctions within the schools or the juvenile justice system had exhausted all other options and needed to complete the program or they would no longer be able to return to school or would find themselves deeper into the juvenile justice system. One counselor noted, "Youth who were on their last strike and really had no other options really stepped out, meaning, they really needed this group to go well, for court, to get back in school, and to get back in the community." Some of the participating youth tended to continue on a path of resisting change until no other alternatives were available. It was evident to the counselors which youth still had options: "They had two more steps they could take before that was it [their last strike]. . . . They did not have a sense of urgency." Youth at the extremes, the younger ones, or those on their "last strike" seemed to be the best candidates for potential change.

Having more serious handgun experiences was another characteristic of youth who seemed to be more open and cooperative. Youth with more serious experiences with handguns were more likely to participate in the lessons. They seemed to understand some of the devastating consequences of carrying or using a handgun. Youth with direct involvement or family involvement in more serious handgun altercations were able to relate to the lessons that counselors were teaching. These youth were able to have a positive influence on others. Their leadership was often enough to turn a group of youth unwilling to listen or participate into a more productive class. In contrast, there were others in the groups who influenced more impressionable youth in a negative manner, disrupting class, and denying responsibility for their behavior.

Finally, parental involvement seemed to be associated with greater openness and cooperation of youth participating in the project. Parental support and reinforcement of the handgun curricula seemed to play an important role for these youth.

Intervention Implementation

Five aspects of the implementation facilitated cooperation from youth. First, speakers who were slightly older and had serious handgun experience seemed to capture the attention of youth. Such speakers were brought in as part of the curriculum to talk about their experiences with handguns. Youth seemed to relate personally to these speakers and appeared more open to learn from them because they understood the youths' life circumstances, their challenges, how to change, and where their lives were going if they did not. In contrast, the textbook scenarios were not as captivating. Agency staff indicated that "youth are not interested in make-believe scenarios; instead, accounts of real statistics, facts, and testimonials grabbed their attention and participation."

Second, discussing the consequences of handgun behavior seemed to engage youth. Understanding the potentially devastating consequences for youth, parents, and victims seemed to sensitize them to the consequences of their actions. These discussions were particularly important because youth engaged in a difficult situation involving handguns tend to focus on their anger, revenge, and threats to their status rather than on the legal consequences of their actions or consequences for others. Further, the general education on the legal consequences of youth carrying and using a handgun reinforced the importance of stopping to think about the consequences. That is, many of the youth knew they should not be carrying or using a handgun, but they were unaware of the specific legal consequences that would result if they were caught.

Third, although an empirical question, service providers felt that a longer intervention period was necessary to promote the desired changes in the youth participating in this project. The curriculum for the school-based program was twenty-five weeks in length, compared to six weeks for the group-based programs. The youth in the school-based program were taught conflict resolution skills, practiced them during class, used them outside of class, and then shared their experiences with the rest of the class. The tell-show-try or modeling technique is an important intervention principle (Gendreau, Bonta, and Cullen, 1994; Sarason and Ganzer, 1980). The length of the program was intended to allow youth time to develop the skills needed for some of the social contexts they would return to every day. However, the quantitative results indicated that the school-based intervention did no better than the group-based interventions. Counselors in the group-based agencies indicated that a six-week curriculum was not long enough. They needed more time to develop rapport with the youth to have an influence on them. A longer time span in terms of weeks, but a shorter class time, was more appropriate for the youth and developing the relationship counselors needed to have with them. As one program provider mentioned, "Two-hour sessions were too long for youth with a forty-five minute attention span." The staff found they needed to "mix up the program a lot during the lessons, using some multimedia, some discussions, and some activities."

Fourth, teachers played an important role in the implementation of the programs, particularly in building trust and rapport. Implementing the curriculum in a class with no known chance of teacher turnover was important. Classes without a consistent teacher did not gain as much active participation. To the extent possible, teachers as well as program staff should commit to participating in the study for the duration of the project or should not be allowed to participate. Emergencies would, of course, be exempt. Not surprisingly, teacher buy-in was also important for program implementation. Teachers who understood the importance of the conflict resolution curriculum seemed to have fewer implementation issues than those who did not. These teachers were also very supportive of the research and were extremely helpful to the researchers or staff when administering questionnaires. Cultural competency on the part of teachers was also important. Having bilingual instructors was crucial when working with predominantly Spanish-speaking youth. Some of the inner-city schools have a large population of Mexican immigrants where English is a second language. Bilingual instructors help to reduce the cultural gap by teaching appropriate conflict resolution and anger management skills in Spanish. Teaching predominantly Spanish-speaking youth in English, again, not surprisingly, was not particularly productive. The intended effect of the interventions was undoubtedly diluted because youth were struggling with the English language while trying to learn new skills.

The fifth aspect of the interventions that helped to facilitate the implementation was the manner in which youth were incorporated into the broader violence prevention services the agencies offered. The handgun violence curriculum reinforced the anger management and conflict resolution concepts taught as part of existing practices. Staff members were well versed in the original violence prevention components and only had the handgun component of the curriculum to learn. Further, the violence prevention interventions had well-established relationships with the referral agencies, schools, and juvenile justice agencies that helped staff build a clientele for this program.

Four aspects of the interventions did not work well. First, counselors in the group-based agencies were often in contact with the youth's probation officer to discuss various issues from compliance to the general status of the case. This contact made the youth apprehensive and increased their resistance. Second, at the beginning of the project, the younger adolescents (aged ten to fourteen) in the group-based agencies were in the same group as older adolescents (aged fifteen to seventeen) because of the small number of referrals. The wide age range was problematic for learning due to differences in levels of risk. Third, increasing the probability of attendance was important; those who did not attend classes for whatever reason clearly would not receive the intended benefits of the interventions. Providing bus tokens, food, and any other incentives for attending class was helpful, but these incentives were not used consistently throughout the project. Finally, agency staff believed the curriculum would be better received by youth if it had less of a handgun violence focus and more of a focus on general violence prevention. Some of the youth, particularly those in the school-based prevention setting, were discouraged by the handgun focus and the lack of variety of the types of violence discussed.

Challenges and Accomplishments

Researchers, program directors, and staff faced programmatic, evaluation, and project challenges. The programmatic challenges included staff turnover and working with youth having violence as a common experience of their everyday lives. These agencies are not adequately funded, even though they are staffed by people with an intrinsic motivation to help. Given these circumstances, it is not surprising that skilled staff went back to school or moved on to other positions for slightly higher pay. Much time was spent on behalf of the agencies and researchers training new staff on programmatic and research protocols. For agencies where most of the staff and the director changed within a short amount of time, there was an overwhelming amount to read, learn, and implement. New staff did the best they could to become oriented and keep progressing. Not a single person in either the school or group-based agencies who started the project—including the agency directors—finished it.

According to the service providers, high-risk youth seemed particularly resistant to change and inattentive unless they were on their "last strike."

They also tended to be more disruptive to the group and more likely to avoid attending classes. Many of the youth were resistant to change, either because of low motivation or because their environment was not conducive to change. Agency staff suggested that the neighborhoods in which many youth live severely impede motivation to change. Their places of residence were not conducive to nonviolent means of settling disputes or affirming themselves among peers. Agency staff brought in presenters raised in similar neighborhoods with whom youth could identify, and they provided situation-specific, adaptive alternatives to handgun carrying that enhance a positive sense of self. However, agency staff reported that the territorial and transactional limits on youth either stifled the internalization of alternative values or provided no opportunities for using learned skills so that self-affirmation and personal safety could be achieved through means other than violence and handgun carrying. Clearly, changing the neighborhood circumstances of youth is vital to the prevention of youth handgun violence, although such an effort would require considerable community resources, mobilization, and political will.

Low motivation to adopt nonviolent methods of managing day-to-day life may reflect the stage of change for many youth in this sample (Giordano, Cernkovich, and Rudolph, 2002; Prochaska, Norcross, and DiClemente, 1995). Some youth may not be ready to modify their attitudes and behavior because they find them appropriate or adaptive to their situation. Handgun attitudes and behaviors may be integral in achieving status and respect among peers. The identity verified from handgun carrying can be deeply rooted, far outweighing the experience of a six-, twelve-, or twenty-five-week handgun violence intervention. Assessing readiness to change and using motivational interviewing techniques that have been promising for other types of behavioral change might be effective in confronting the difficult challenge of changing youth handgun attitudes and behaviors (Miller and Rollnick, 2002).

Additionally, the two agencies using group settings for counseling or life skills training might have inadvertently become training grounds for delinquency and violence. For example, Dishion, McCord, and Poulin (1999) reported evidence suggesting "iatrogenic effects" in peer-group interventions, where high-risk youth often support one another's criminal or delinquent behavior. The point is consistent with the counter-intuitive findings in this study concerning handgun carrying as well as the qualitative accounts of challenges faced by agency staff in managing such groups. Dishion and others (1999, p. 11) claim "youth being actively reinforced through laughter, social attention, and interest for deviant behavior are likely to increase such behavior." Such reinforcement processes are consistent with the challenges described by agency staff where high-risk youth were often disruptive to the group and challenging to manage. These findings imply that caution should be exercised when contemplating peer group-based interventions with high-risk youth, with group composition being an important consideration.

To the extent that neighborhoods marked by disadvantaged circumstances for the healthy development of youth persist, interventions designed to reduce the incentive for youth to arm themselves are likely to have limited if any effect. This is particularly the case if handguns become symbols of power and control, fostering a positive identity in youth having limited access to conventional means for achieving that developmental milestone. Once identity is rooted in violence and firearms, the deep roots become difficult to extricate.

The lack of motivation resulted in low attendance and a lack of interest and participation. These youth were still in a pre-contemplative or contemplative stage of change, as opposed to the preparation, action, or maintenance stages (Prochaska, Norcross, and DiClemente, 1995). That is, they were not motivated to learn conflict resolution and anger management skills because they believed nothing was wrong with their current method of solving conflict and they were achieving the goals and status they needed in their environment. No other ways to solve conflicts seemed realistic. Stopping to think about the consequences of their behavior or taking deep breaths to calm down in a dangerous neighborhood could result in severe unintended consequences. Returning to the context of their lives was the problem, an issue agencies could not directly address. In cases where the context was not so dangerous, implementing new skills could be supplemented by solutions offered by speakers who were once in the youths' situation and could talk them through approaches that might work in their neighborhoods.

These programmatic challenges were compounded by simultaneous challenges with evaluation protocols. Several evaluation challenges resulted from the program staff's lack of experience with evaluation protocols and the difficult nature of obtaining six-month post-tests from youth. First, obtaining parental consent was a challenge for both the school-based and group-based agencies. For school-based agencies, parental consent forms needed to be sent home well in advance, two to three weeks generally, and with many reminders to bring them back. The group-based agencies found the best time to obtain consent for the research project was at intake rather than at a subsequent meeting, despite initial intentions to wait. Agency staff initially believed that introducing the study and completing the pre-test questionnaire was inappropriate at intake. However, it became evident that youth and parents were not likely to return forms that were sent home, and there was no other time more conducive to achieving the task more efficiently. Second, staff members from both the school-based and group-based programs were challenged by using identification numbers rather than names to keep information confidential. Many meetings between agency staff and the researchers were held to make sure that the youth and parent pre-tests matched the post-tests. Patience, understanding, and humor from both the researchers and the agency staff were important to keep the evaluation moving along, particularly during times of staff turnover.

Third, the evaluation tasks were also time consuming for the agency staff who were not paid for the additional tasks and were often overworked due to a lack of funding in general for violence prevention programming. Locating youth six months after they started their participation for the post-test proved to be quite difficult, requiring more time than expected. Finding accurate or current phone numbers and addresses for this transient population was the most difficult aspect of this task. Once accurate contact information was found, repeated telephone and personal contacts were required to obtain the post-tests needed. As a result, some agencies assigned two staff members to evaluation tasks in order to complete the data collection. Researchers helped to alleviate the evaluation challenges by offering and encouraging agency staff to ask for additional help when needed. Despite the challenges, staff made every effort to follow research protocols and complete the post-testing needed for the project. More intense training could have helped decrease some of the evaluation challenges as well as some of the overall project challenges.

Agency staff recommended longer training sessions or workshops on the evaluation protocols to enhance their understanding and the skills needed to complete the evaluation tasks as designed. A few hours of training and written instructions were insufficient for the staff to gain a full understanding of the project and the evaluation protocols. Hands-on evaluation training involving an introduction to evaluation, practice completing the information on the evaluation forms, using the corresponding parent forms, and completing the Excel spreadsheets would have also been helpful in alleviating some of the evaluation challenges.

There were also several overall project challenges. First, new agency staff requested an official orientation to the project. A meeting with new staff, describing the project history and providing reading materials, was insufficient. Rather, a longer, structured orientation with a presentation of the literature review on youth handgun violence, the project history, and a project manual was needed. Such training was difficult to accomplish in a short project period and in a situation where the interventions and evaluations were not specified prior to the beginning of the project. That is, the interventions and evaluation protocols were developed as part of the project. Although the evolving nature of the project had its advantages, such as a greater tendency to bridge research and practice rather than impose research on practice, there were other disadvantages. Setbacks in starting the interventions occurred due to a delay in the human subject approval of the research protocols. This was particularly difficult for the school-based program, as it is restricted to a school calendar, making it difficult to delay a twenty-five-week curriculum. For school-based programs, a six-month planning phase starting in January is more practical than starting the planning phase in July. That is, the project's six-month planning phase started in July and ended in December with only a short period between the time the human subjects proposal could be written and submitted and the time schools would preferably have liked to start the curriculum. Having the summer break instead of the winter break to obtain human subject clearance would have made for a better transition from the planning phase to the pilot or implementation phase. A longer project time overall may alleviate some of these challenges. Three years was not enough time to develop, pilot, implement, and evaluate a handgun violence prevention effort.

Second, the pilot phase of the project was challenging but important for the agencies as well as for the researchers. Agencies were allowed to make changes to their interventions, modifying aspects that did not appear to be working well. For example, some of the materials disseminated to the youth from the speakers in the group-based programs on the current handgun laws were especially difficult for the youth or parents to understand. It was important to modify the information from formal statutes on handgun behavior to a document with a more accessible level of reading and comprehension. These adjustments were easy compared to finding schools to participate in a handgun violence prevention project. Despite assurance of confidentiality, schools were reluctant to engage in a project that was handgun related or that might suggest they had a handgun violence issue, particularly after the tragic events at Columbine High School. Schools were also challenged by a state requirement to achieve adequate testing scores for the Colorado Student Assessment Program (CSAP). Schools were more inclined to spend time ensuring youth did well on the CSAP than including a curriculum on conflict resolution or handgun violence prevention. One principal noted that "it is too much to ask for a school to give up twenty-five class periods for anything other than academics." In contrast, schools with youth caught for weapon violations were happy to refer them to an outside agency such as the group-based agencies to receive handgun violence intervention. Youth completing such an intervention could be reintegrated into school after being expelled.

The pilot phase was also important to researchers for assessments of test instruments and for discovering the importance of incentives. Families and youth preferred one type of incentive over others, such as pizza parties for youth or gift certificates at local markets. This phase also served to facilitate communication between the researchers and the agency staff, assisting in the integration of the evaluation activities and the intervention activities.

After the implementation phase, agency staff and directors could cite many accomplishments. They were proud of being able to reach a group of youth they would not have otherwise reached. After the completion of the group-based interventions, youth who were expelled for a weapon violation were able to go back to school. Additionally, an intuitive sense of accomplishing intervention goals among the agency staff was realized when certain youth "turned their lives around." One youth wrote the following journal entry: "In today's class I realized that I am at risk of being shot with every step that I take. My brother's friend was shot in the chest and is barely recovering after a year and a half. I am now more open to the possibilities that can happen to me everyday. I used to have a gun, but now I don't, and I am happy that I got rid of it." Another youth reported making the choice to stop attending parties where there might be gangs, handguns, or violence. Additionally, over the course of the project, many students reported to staff that they had successfully used nonviolent skills with parents, teachers, friends, and siblings. In some cases, youth who were successful in changing their lives would serve as speakers for subsequent handgun violence groups.

Working relationships were also developed among staff from the agencies, schools, and other youth service agencies as a result of the project. These relationships were evident in the project meetings and were particularly helpful to the different agencies because of the communication and collaboration that occurred. The project meeting often served as a forum for discussing challenges and exchanging solutions. The communication between the agency staff facilitated project progress as they helped each other get through each stage of the project.

Despite the challenges, agency staff learned how to participate in a quasi-experimental design, made every effort to complete the necessary tasks, and were pleased with being able to finish the evaluation. They were often new to evaluation protocols, where consent forms were required, intervention changes during the evaluation were prohibited, and confidential data collection protocols were followed. The learning curve was steep, but agency staff succeeded in the difficult task of completing the evaluation of their interventions.

Summary and Conclusion

The qualitative observations captured characteristics of youth who seemed to be more open and receptive to the interventions, aspects of implementation that went well, and challenges and accomplishments. Characteristics of youth associated with a greater willingness to participate included younger age groups, those still in school, those motivated to do well because of their lack of alternative options in school or the juvenile justice system, youth experiencing the serious consequences of handgun use, and those where parents were involved. Aspects of program implementation that seemed desirable to the agency staff included using outside speakers to whom youth could relate yet who challenged the youths' thinking patterns, discussing the consequences of handgun behavior, interventions of greater duration, and culturally competent, stable teachers with program buy-in. Staff turnover and engaging youth at highest risk of violence were the main challenges faced during the project. Evaluation challenges resulted from agency staff's lack of experience with evaluation protocols, obtaining six-month post-tests from youth, and recruiting schools to participate in a handgun violence project. Finally, the staff felt a qualitative sense of accomplishment for working with youth engaging in handgun violence. They were able to see a few youth turn their lives around, collaborative relationships were developed as a result of the project, and they succeeded in the difficult task of completing the evaluation of their programs. Despite the disappointing research findings of the evaluation, the collaboration between the community-based agencies, the private foundation supporting this effort, and the evaluation team was successful and provided a "learning laboratory" for future collaborative prevention and evaluation projects.

References

Dishion, T. J., McCord, J., and Poulin, F. "When Interventions Harm: Peer Groups and Problem Behavior." *American Psychologist,* 1999, *54*(9), 755–764.

Gendreau, P., Bonta, J., and Cullen, F. T. "Intensive Rehabilitation Supervision: The Next Generation in Community Corrections." *Federal Probation,* 1994, *58,* 72–78.

Giordano, P. C., Cernkovich, S. A., and Rudolph, J. L. "Gender, Crime, and Desistance: Toward a Theory of Cognitive Transformation." *American Journal of Sociology,* 2002, *107,* 990–1064.

Miller, W. R., and Rollnick, S. *Motivational Interviewing: Preparing People for Change.* New York: Guilford Press, 2002.

Prochaska, J. O., Norcross, J. C., and DiClemente, C. C. *Changing for Good.* New York: Avon Books, 1995.

Sarason, I. G., and Ganzer, V. J. "Modeling and Group Discussion in the Rehabilitation of Juvenile Delinquents." In R. R. Ross and P. Gendreau (eds.), *Effective Correctional Treatment.* Toronto, Canada: Butterworth, 1980.

Williams, K. R., and Arredondo Mattson, S. "Determinants of Handgun Attitudes and Handgun Behaviors among Urban Youth." Paper presented at the annual meeting of the American Society of Criminology, Chicago, Ill., 2002.

Williams, K. R., and Arredondo Mattson, S. "Access to Handguns Among Urban Youth: Attitudinal and Behavioral Implications." Paper presented at annual meeting of the American Society of Criminology, Denver, Colo., 2003.

KIRK R. WILLIAMS is professor of sociology and associate director at the Robert Presley Center for Crime and Justice Studies at the University of California, Riverside.

SABRINA ARREDONDO MATTSON is senior research associate at National Research Center in Boulder, Colorado.

2

This chapter describes potential drawbacks of using intent-to-treat (ITT) analyses to examine intervention effects and presents several additional analytic methods as alternatives to ITT.

Masked Intervention Effects: Analytic Methods for Addressing Low Dosage of Intervention

John E. Lochman, Caroline Boxmeyer, Nicole Powell, David L. Roth, Michael Windle

This chapter examines how a particular strategy for analyzing evaluation data, intent-to-treat analyses, may underestimate the true effects of interventions. Such underestimation of intervention effects can profoundly influence policies for prevention and treatment of children's mental health problems, which can in turn lead to negative consequences for children's healthy development. However, evaluating treatment is a complicated issue because poorer outcomes for some may be due to characteristics of the participants, such as low motivation or chaotic family conditions, rather than qualities of the intervention. Intent-to-treat analyses purposely ignore these nonrandom sources of variance.

Using intent-to-treat analyses, evaluations of programs to reduce oppositional defiant disorders and conduct disorders in children and adolescents have consistently revealed that cognitive-behavioral interventions have the most promise and clearest evidence for efficacy, with effect sizes on outcome analyses in the moderate to large range (from .3 to over 1.0) (Brestan and Eyberg, 1998; Leff and others, 2001). These interventions usually involve

Note: This study was funded by a grant provided by the Centers for Disease Control and Prevention (R49<\\>CCR418569). Additional support was provided by grants from the National Institute of Drug Abuse (DA-08453, DA-16135).

NEW DIRECTIONS FOR EVALUATION, no. 110, Summer 2006   © Wiley Periodicals, Inc.
Published online in Wiley InterScience (www.interscience.wiley.com) • DOI: 10.1002/ev.184

19

behavioral parent training but also can include social problem-solving skills training, anger management training, and social skills training with the children (Lochman and others, 2001).

Coping Power Program: An Evidence-Based Program for Aggressive Children

Using the Coping Power Program (Lochman, Wells, and Murray, forthcoming) as an example of an evidence-based program for aggressive children, this chapter compares alternative analysis strategies for program evaluation. Coping Power, a multicomponent prevention program, includes school-based weekly sessions for children that focus on enhancing and reinforcing goal setting, organizational skills, emotional awareness, anger management skills, accurate attributions of others' intentions, social problem-solving skills, and resistance to peer pressure. In concert with the child sessions, parents are invited to twice-monthly parent group sessions, typically in the afternoons or evenings at the children's schools. These parent sessions address child behavior management, stress management for parents, and communication and problem-solving for families.

Randomized, controlled evaluation studies indicate that the Coping Power intervention has broad effects at post-intervention on boys' social information processing and locus of control and on parents' socialization practices (Lochman and Wells, 2002b). At one-year follow-ups with two separate samples, Coping Power significantly reduced self-reported delinquency, parent-reported substance use, and teacher-reported behavioral problems, especially for boys who received both the child and parent components (Lochman and Wells, 2003, 2004). Perhaps most important, these outcome effects were mediated through changes in children's social reasoning and parents' management of their children's behavior (Lochman and Wells, 2002a). Therefore, parental participation in training can significantly affect the magnitude of program effects.

Parent Attendance and Dosage Effects in the Coping Power Program

In the Coping Power evaluation studies, children sustained high levels of participation, with session attendance rates typically at 90 percent or higher. However, attendance at parent sessions was highly variable. Because parents are invited into the program rather than initiating the contact (as would be true in mental health treatment settings), some parents are only minimally engaged. A substantial minority of parents never attends any of the parents' sessions, and overall parent attendance at sessions has ranged from 30 percent to 50 percent across Coping Power evaluations. However, a number of program strategies encourage parental attendance (Lochman and Wells, 1996), including sessions scheduled at convenient times (such as after

5 P.M. to accommodate working parents' schedules), meetings in parents' neighborhoods, small grant-funded stipends for parents who attend, child-care provided on site, and dinner or snacks for parents and children. In addition, program staff send home reminder letters and make reminder telephone calls prior to each parent meeting. Despite these efforts, parent attendance has remained modest in all of the evaluation studies to date.

This issue of less-than-adequate compliance to treatment has been recognized as an important concern in mental health services research on dose response (Foster, 2003). Research on whether attendance rates and dosage have an effect on treatment outcomes with children and adolescents in community mental health service settings has produced mixed results. For example, the Fort Bragg Evaluation Study found no relationship between the number of outpatient treatment contacts in a managed care system and children's improvement (Andrade, Lambert, and Bickman, 2000). However, using alternative analysis strategies, Foster (2003) found that added levels of services did improve treatment outcome in children's behavioral functioning. Other research also indicates that dosage can make a difference in outcome. Angold and others (2000) found that the number of sessions received by children in rural mental health clinics in the Smoky Mountains study related significantly to improved symptoms at follow-up. Finally, and most importantly for our example, some parent training studies find that children whose parents attend more regularly have better outcomes than those whose parents attend fewer sessions (Reid, Webster-Stratton, and Baydar, 2004). This research suggests that attendance, particularly for parents, may have substantial impact on evaluation findings for intervention programs.

Analytic Approaches that Address Varying Levels of Intervention Attendance

Intent-to-Treat (ITT). ITT analyses for program evaluations with randomized experimental designs provide rigorous tests of intervention effects. Once cases are randomized to conditions, all cases are included in analyses. Although this is a widely accepted analytic strategy, estimates of intervention effect sizes can be biased if any participants fail to comply with the assigned treatment condition (Jo and Muthén, 2001). In our example with the Coping Power Program, bias would result if attendance at parent sessions varies among parents. ITT compares average outcomes between randomized groups, but ignores compliance. An ITT analysis provides evidence of whether the intervention and control groups differ, but if significant intervention effects are not detected, it remains unclear if the intervention was ineffective or if non-compliance with the intervention undermined its estimated efficacy. Essentially, ITT evaluates the effects of randomization rather than the effect of the intervention itself (Yau and Little, 2001). This concern has resulted in efforts to develop alternative analytic methods (Dunn and others, 2003), and such alternatives are particularly important for interventions that may involve high rates of non-compliance.

As-Treated Analyses. An early alternative method for handling low rates of attendance in mental health interventions has been to set a threshold for compliance and then to compare only those in the intervention condition who have received the adequate dose ("compliers") to the entire control group, or more rarely to the control group plus the low-dose intervention individuals (Jo and Muthén, 2001). However, the selective deletion of low-dose intervention participants ("non-compliers") undermines the advantages of randomization (Yau and Little, 2001) and produces a selection bias in outcome analyses. For example, in evaluations of Coping Power, non-compliers likely vary in a variety of ways from compliers, including parents' ability to perceive children's problem behaviors accurately and their motivation to change those behaviors. Unfortunately, the simple approach of deleting non-compliers from the analysis usually results in a comparison of a select group of intervention participants who possess certain characteristics (for example, high motivation) to the full control group that includes individuals who vary in those specific characteristics (for example, have high and low motivation). Thus, if group differences are found, it may be due to variations in parents' motivation to try to change their children's behavior rather than to the intervention.

Propensity Scores. This approach matches compliant intervention participants with similar individuals in the control group on multiple observed covariates (D'Agostino, 1998; Rubin, 1997; Frangakis and Rubin, 2002). The statistical procedure reduces a set of baseline (background) characteristics into a composite score that can be used to represent the probability of being a compliant intervention participant. These probabilities, or propensity scores, for the compliant intervention participants are then matched at a case level with propensity scores for individuals in the control condition. This permits a comparison between compliers in the intervention condition with individuals in the control condition who, on the basis of similar baseline data, likely would have complied with the intervention had it been assigned to them.

There are several approaches to matching the propensity scores of compliers in the intervention and control conditions, and some authors implement more than one approach (Hill, Brooks-Gunn, and Waldfogel, 2003). The greedy matching technique is a recently refined approach that was developed to balance the sometimes competing goals of maximizing the exactness of the matches and maximizing the number of cases that can be matched (Parsons, 2001). In the greedy matching technique, an iterative matching algorithm is used to match as many cases as possible at the fifth decimal point of the propensity score, then to the fourth decimal point, and so on down to the first decimal point. Once a match is identified, both participants are removed from the remaining pool of participants, although some investigators have used matching-with-replacement procedures in which the same control may be selected as a match for multiple intervention participants (for example, Hill, Brooks-Gunn, and Waldfogel, 2003). When the greedy matching technique is used without replacement, inevitably some compliant intervention participants cannot be matched to a control at the first decimal place, and these cases are then excluded from subsequent intervention versus control comparisons.

Complier Average Causal Effect (CACE). The CACE method has been developed as another approach to dealing with problems introduced by non-compliance (Angrist, Imbens, and Rubin, 1996). CACE begins with an assumption that treatment has no effect among non-compliers and uses an instrumental variable approach (Bloom, 1984) or structural equation modeling procedures (Jo and Muthén, 2001) to estimate the unobserved variable of compliance in the control group. Intervention compliers and control individuals who would have been compliant with the intervention had it been offered to them are then compared to estimate the true effects of treatment among the compliers (Dunn and others, 2003). Estimates of the unobserved compliance variable among the controls may be more precise when baseline covariates are added to the model, but CACE models can also be run with no covariates.

Although propensity score approaches and CACE approaches offer considerable advantages over the as-treated method, they might be seen as supplements to traditional ITT analysis that maintains the methodological advantages of complete randomization. Whereas ITT completely ignores compliance, both propensity score approaches and CACE approaches take compliance into account, although usually as a simple dichotomy (compliant versus non-compliant) or into a few categorical levels (Ialongo, Poduska, Werthamer, and Kellam, 2001). By separating compliance rates from estimates of treatment effects among the compliant, these alternative methods are able to clarify the mechanisms by which some interventions may fail to demonstrate significant treatment effects using conventional ITT methods.

Comparison Among Methods for Addressing Differences in Compliance

Although progress is being made in developing and using new methods for addressing variable levels of participant attendance in intervention trials, these methods have rarely been compared and have not been applied at all to preventive interventions designed to reduce children's problem behaviors. Using analyses of the effects of an intervention designed to reduce children's externalizing behavior problems and thus their risk for later delinquency and substance use as an example, we will compare how propensity analyses and three types of CACE analyses fare in comparison to traditional ITT analyses and often-used as-treated analyses. Although these techniques have been presented as an alternative and possible improvement,

NEW DIRECTIONS FOR EVALUATION • DOI: 10.1002/ev

analyses of compliance have not considered the consequences of how the criteria for compliance are determined for a particular intervention, nor do they account for whether the compliance analyses produce different effects at different levels of compliance. Therefore, the present example will also compare two levels of compliance, one representing a criterion of at least minimal compliance with the intervention and a second representing a high level of attendance and compliance.

Project Description

In the administration of the abbreviated Coping Power Program used for this example, 240 aggressive fifth grade boys (64 percent) and girls (36 percent) identified as at-risk for delinquent behavior were randomly assigned to either the Coping Power intervention (n = 120) or to a no-treatment control condition (n = 120). Participants were selected who were rated as being in the top 30 percent of fourth grade students on teacher ratings of aggressive behavior. Eighty-five percent of the families initially contacted agreed to participate, resulting in the total sample of 240. The analyses below report on the 224 participants (n = 112 in each condition) for whom complete outcome data are available. The gender and racial or ethnic distribution and family composition were similar across participants in the intervention and control conditions. Sixty-nine percent of the children self-identified as African American, 30 percent as Caucasian, and 1 percent as other race or ethnicity. The largest group (40 percent) consisted of children living with a single mother; 29 percent lived with both biological parents, 19 percent with their mother and another adult male, 8 percent with other relatives, and 4 percent in an out-of-home placement. Thirty-seven percent of the families reported an annual income of less than $15,000, 26 percent between $15,000 and $29,000, 22 percent between $30,000 and $49,000, and 15 percent greater than $50,000.

The Coping Power Program is a manualized cognitive behavioral preventive intervention for youth at risk for behavior problems (Lochman, Wells, and Murray, forthcoming). The current study assessed an abbreviated version of the program that included twenty-four child group sessions and ten parent group sessions (Lochman, 2003). Each child and parent group was co-led by two members of the research team, typically one doctoral-level and one master's-level staff member. The child groups, conducted at seven participating elementary schools, consisted of five to six children and focused on teaching coping and problem solving skills as well as strategies for enhancing social relationships and resisting peer pressure. The parent groups included parents and primary caregivers of the target children and focused on teaching behavior management skills and improving family problem solving, communication, and cohesion. The children assigned to the intervention condition received nearly the full dose of the Coping Power Child Component, with an overall attendance level of 93 percent. Parent attendance was much more erratic, with 30 percent of parents not attending any of the ten sessions offered. The mean number of Coping Power parent sessions attended was 3.76 (SD = 3.58; range 0 to 10).

Intervention effects were assessed using teacher ratings of externalizing behavior problems on the Behavior Assessment System for Children-Teacher Rating Scale (BASC-TRS; Reynolds and Kamphaus, 1992). The externalizing composite scale provides a summary measure of hyperactivity, conduct problems, and aggressive behavior and has strong internal consistency (Cronbach's alpha = .96 at both pre- and post-intervention). Intervention outcomes were assessed by examining change in teacher-rated externalizing behavior problems from pre- to post-intervention, after controlling for baseline externalizing behavior problems.

Analytic Methods

Four general types of models were specified and evaluated. First, an intention-to-treat (ITT) analysis was conducted that compared the 112 participants randomly assigned to the Coping Power Program with the 112 participants randomly assigned to the control condition. A second analytic approach involved comparing only the compliers at each threshold with all of the controls. The third analytic approach used propensity scores to match Coping Power compliers at both thresholds with selected controls. Thirteen variables measured at baseline (gender, teacher-rated externalizing problems of the child, parent-rated externalizing problems of the child, parental depression, parental involvement, cohesive family relations, parental aggressive problem solving, life stressors, community supportiveness, child anger toward peers, child revenge goals, child temperamental activity level, and child perceived competence in interactions with peers) were used in a binary logistic regression model to estimate the probability of being a complier versus a control. The five-to-one greedy matching procedures (Parsons, 2001) were then used to match individual compliers with individual controls. (Information on the baseline covariate variables can be obtained from the first author.)

For our fourth general analytic approach, we specified a Complier Average Causal Effect (CACE) model. Although compliance status is an observed variable for the participants in an active treatment program, it is an unobserved (or latent) classification variable for the controls. The CACE approach estimates this latent class variable on the basis of the observed outcomes of all participants and the predictors of compliance in the active treatment group. A key assumption of the CACE model is that the non-compliers in the treatment group have the same outcomes as those in the control group who would have been non-compliers had they been assigned to the treatment group.

Of the one hundred twelve Coping Power intervention participants, a parent for seventy-nine of these participants (70.5 percent) attended at least one session and was considered one of the compliers in the first set of analyses, leaving thirty-three cases where the parents did not attend any sessions and were therefore classified as non-compliers. For the second set of analyses, a higher compliance threshold of eight sessions was used, indicating that the parent had received the bulk of the information presented in the ten parent group sessions, and the twenty-seven parents (24.1 percent) who attended eight or more sessions were considered compliers, compared to the 85 cases considered non-compliers because a parent did not attend at least eight sessions.

The results of the analytic models are summarized in Table 2.1. The column labeled as "estimate" represents the difference between the Coping Power Program and the control group for changes on the teacher externalizing score. In the ITT model, for example, the decreases observed on the teacher externalizing score were 3.69 units greater, on average, for those assigned to Coping Power than for those assigned to the control condition after controlling for the influence of baseline score on this variable. This ITT effect closely approached conventional levels of statistical significance ($p = .056$). Statistically significant effects were found when the 33 cases who were assigned to the Coping Power Program but failed to attend at least one session were excluded from the analysis, leaving only compliers ($n = 79$) versus all controls ($p = .041$). The propensity score matching procedure resulted in control matches for sixty-four of the seventy-nine Coping Power participants who attended at least one session (81 percent of intervention compliers were successfully matched), and a comparison of these sixty-four Coping Power participants with the sixty-four controls resulted in a highly significant difference between treatment compliers and matched controls ($p = .009$).

Table 2.1. Comparison of Approaches for Addressing Variable Parent Attendance in Intervention

Model	Estimate	SE	t	p
Intention-to-treat	−3.690	1.919	−1.92	.056
Compliance Threshold = 1 session:				
Compliers vs. controls	−4.316	2.093	−2.06	.041
Propensity score—greedy matching	−6.292	2.367	−2.66	.009
CACE—Baseline covariate only	−4.707	2.391	−1.97	.048
CACE—All covariates	−3.461	2.450	−1.41	.158
CACE—Backward elimination of covariates	−4.234	2.381	−1.78	.075
Compliance Threshold = 8 sessions:				
Compliers vs. controls	−5.431	2.857	−1.90	.059
Propensity score—greedy matching	−3.956	3.827	−1.03	.307
CACE—Baseline covariate only	−12.77	12.624	−1.01	.312
CACE—All covariates	−0.769	3.495	−0.22	.826
CACE—Backward elimination of covariates	−2.537	3.585	−0.71	.479

In CACE models, the analyst has flexibility in deciding whether baseline covariates will be modeled as predictors of outcome, compliance status, or both. Three different CACE models were tested at each compliance threshold on the basis of these options. In the "baseline covariate only" model, the baseline teacher externalizing score was modeled as a predictor of change in teacher externalizing score, but no other covariates were included and no covariates were modeled as predictors of compliance. In the "all covariates" model, all thirteen covariates used in the propensity score calculation were entered as predictors of both outcome and compliance status. In the "backward elimination of covariates" model, nonsignificant covariate effects on both outcome and compliance were deleted from the "all covariates" model until only statistically significant effects remained in the model.

As Table 2.1 indicates, the simple model with baseline teacher externalizing score included as the only covariate of outcome provided a statistically significant difference between treatment compliers and controls who would have been compliers (p = .048). The effect after backward elimination of covariates also approached statistical significance (p = .075). In the backward elimination model, both baseline teacher-rated externalizing (p < .001) and perceived competence with peers (p = .014) were significant predictors of outcome while parent involvement was the only statistically significant predictor of compliance (p < .001).

For the compliance threshold of eight sessions, only the analyses that compared these compliers (27 of the 112 randomized to Coping Power) with all the controls approached statistical significance (p = .059). Twenty-two of these 27 compliers had propensity score matches in the control group (81 percent of intervention compliers using this definition of compliance were successfully matched to control participants), but the direct comparison of these 44 subjects failed to achieve statistical significance. Also, all CACE models yielded non-significant differences between the 27 compliers and those in the control group who would have theoretically complied at this high level. In the backward elimination model, both baseline teacher externalizing score (p < .001) and perceived peer competence (p < .01) predicted outcome, while perceived peer competence, parent involvement, revenge social goals, life stressors, and parental aggressive problem solving all predicted compliance status (p < .05). Higher scores on parental involvement were associated with greater compliance, whereas higher scores on the other four predictors were associated with a lower likelihood of compliance.

Implications for Program Evaluation

The general conclusion from comparing these multiple analysis strategies is that how one specifies parents' compliance in an evaluation design for a preventive intervention, as indicated in this example by the degree of parent attendance in parent sessions, affects the interpretation of findings of program efficacy. Using traditional and rigorous intention-to-treat (ITT) analyses, this intervention, an abbreviated form of the Coping Power Program, tended to produce reductions in teachers' ratings of children's externalizing behavior problems at post-intervention assessments, but the effect only approached conventional levels of statistical significance. However, when parents' compliance to the parent component of the intervention was modeled, the intervention produced statistically significant reductions in children's externalizing behavior among those who complied with the intervention. It is notable that parent attendance had an effect on an outcome from a different source, in this case, teachers' ratings.

Intent-to-treat analyses provide a strong and clear test of whether participants who are randomized to an intervention differ from randomly assigned controls at the close of the intervention. However, because those who have been randomly assigned may not participate in an intervention at equal rates, the ITT provides a conservative, and potentially erroneously low, estimate of the actual effects of an intervention. In prevention research with children, the concern about variable parent participation rates can be especially noteworthy because parents do not initiate participation in a preventive intervention as they would if they were actively seeking treatment for perceived problems with their children. As a result, parent motivation in preventive interventions can be highly variable. There can be a subset of parents whose children are randomly assigned to treatment but have no motivation or intention to become actively involved themselves in intervention sessions. Thus, ITT analyses can present particular challenges for prevention research.

Unfortunately, efforts to account for parents' level of attendance at intervention sessions deviate from the strict assumptions of the randomized control group design. However, several methods tested here reduce the risk of bias due to loss of randomization by carefully matching intervention and control participants. The most naive effort to control for parent attendance compares compliant intervention participants to the entire control group. This approach has the unfortunate effect of including poorly motivated participants in the control group but not in the intervention group, potentially confounding intervention and motivation in a manner that favors the intervention condition. As we have demonstrated in our example, the intervention effect is significant in the as-treated analyses for the low-level compliance comparisons, but this could easily be a biased and erroneous finding. Subsequent propensity and CACE analyses indicate that the intervention effect is indeed statistically significant when a low threshold for parent compliance is considered. However, in the examination of effects using the high threshold for parent compliance, the trend for an intervention effect using the as-treated analyses was not supported by the propensity or CACE analyses. In comparison to the high-compliance threshold analyses, the results for the as-treated analyses appear to be spurious.

NEW DIRECTIONS FOR EVALUATION • DOI: 10.1002/ev

The two approaches that compare minimally compliant intervention participants to control participants who are estimated to be minimally compliant find that the intervention significantly reduced children's externalizing behavior problems. The results indicate the utility of both the propensity score approach and the CACE approach to address participant attendance and compliance. Propensity analyses using the greedy matching technique appear to be a particularly useful method for controlling for differential levels of parent attendance in interventions. CACE analyses make an assumption that a portion of the control group, similar in size to the group of noncompliant intervention children, would be noncompliant, and hence can be estimated to have the same amount of behavior change as the noncompliant individuals in the intervention group. In contrast, propensity score approaches match individuals who are estimated to be similar according to a defined set of baseline characteristics and make no assumptions about the equivalence of noncompliant participants across intervention and control groups on the outcome variable. A primary disadvantage of the propensity score analysis is that not all intervention participants can usually be matched to control participants unless there is a relatively large pool of control participants and a large control-to-intervention participant ratio. However, even with the modest sample size in our example study and the loss of 20 percent of intervention participants during the propensity score matching procedure, the propensity score matching method permitted a useful and informative evaluation of the intervention among the participants who showed at least some level of compliance with the intervention.

The range of outcome results with the three versions of the CACE analyses suggests that the inclusion of a larger number of covariates in CACE analyses had counterproductive results. Unlike the propensity score approach, which typically uses many covariates to arrive at a single propensity score per person and then matches on only this one propensity score, the CACE approach includes the multiple covariates simultaneously in the same model that is examining intervention effects on outcome. This may undermine power for tests of covariate-adjusted predictive effects and open up the possibility of complications such as multicollinearity among the multiple covariates. Unless the covariates can account for a large portion of the variance in the latent compliance construct or in the outcome, the loss of power and exposure to chance variation due to model over-specification may be considerable, especially for relatively small samples. This apparently occurred in our analysis example when all thirteen covariates were specified and estimated for both outcome and compliance in our full CACE model. With small and moderate-sized samples, it may be preferable to select a relatively small number of highly influential covariates if the preferred strategy is a CACE analysis. Because the propensity score summarizes multiple covariates in a single composite score used to match intervention and control cases before conducting the analysis of intervention effects, multiple covariates in the propensity score approach do not have the same effect on the statistical power of the intervention effect as can be the case in CACE models.

Finally, the difference in outcomes when compliers were defined at two criterion levels has considerable practical importance for evaluation. Had we constrained our definition of compliance to only those parents receiving almost the complete intervention, neither the propensity analyses nor the CACE analyses of evaluation data would have supported intervention effects. However, when compliance criteria were set at a level indicating that parents were sufficiently motivated to become involved in a portion of the parenting component, intervention effects were apparent for their children. In the case of our current example, parent involvement in at least a portion of the parenting intervention appears to be important in reducing children's externalizing behavior problems. However, parents apparently do not have to attend nearly all of the sessions to have positive effects. This finding may be explained in part because parents may complete a high dose of the program for very different reasons: because they are enthusiastically committed to learning as much as they can about positive parenting techniques or because they are having modest or no success in altering the behavior of difficult children.

These differences in findings when compliance thresholds were set at different levels suggest that intervention researchers need to work with program designers to carefully estimate the minimally important level of participation necessary for program success. These estimates of thresholds for compliance should be based on theory and the accumulation of empirical results. Future research should aggressively pursue methods for setting optimal thresholds in analytic approaches that extend beyond ITT. However, if this issue is ignored, compliance analyses will run similar risks of providing erroneous results about the effect of interventions.

References

Andrade, A. R., Lambert, E. W., and Bickman, L. "Dose Effect in Psychotherapy: Outcomes Associated with Negligible Treatment." *Journal of the American Academy of Child and Adolescent Psychiatry*, 2000, *39*(2), 161–168.

Angold, A. E., Costello, J., Burns, B. J., Erkanli, A., and Farmer, E.M.Z. "Effectiveness of Nonresidential Specialty Mental Health Services for Children and Adolescents in the 'Real World.'" *Journal of the American Academy of Child and Adolescent Psychiatry*, 2000, *39*(2), 154–160.

Angrist, J. D., Imbens, G. W., and Rubin, D. "Identification of Causal Effects Using Instrumental Variables." *Journal of the American Statistical Association*, 1996, *91*(434), 444–472.

Bloom, H. S. "Accounting for No-Shows in Experimental Evaluation Designs." *Evaluation Review*, 1984, *8*, 225–246.

Brestan, E. V., and Eyberg, S. M. "Effective Psychosocial Treatments of Conduct-Disordered Children and Adolescents: 29 Years, 82 Studies, and 5,272 Kids." *Journal of Clinical Child Psychology*, 1998, *27*(2), 180–189.

D'Agostino, R. B. "Propensity Score Methods for Bias Reduction in the Comparison of a Treatment to a Non-Randomized Control Group." *Statistics in Medicine,* 1998, *17,* 2265–2281.

Dunn, G., Maracy, M., Dowrick, C., Ayuso-Mateos, J. L., Dalgard, O. S., Page, H., Lehtinen, V., Casey, P., Wilkinson, C., Vazquez-Barquero, J. L., and Wilkinson, G. on behalf of the ODIN group. "Estimating Psychological Treatment Effects from a Randomized Controlled Trial with Both Non-compliance and Loss to Follow-up." *British Journal of Psychiatry,* 2003, *183*(4), 323–331.

Foster, E. M. "Propensity Score Matching: An Illustrative Analysis of Dose Response." *Medical Care,* 2003, *41*(10), 1183–1192.

Frangakis, C. E., and Rubin, D. B. "Principal Stratification in Causal Inference." *Biometrics,* 2002, *58*(1), 21–29.

Hill, J. L., Brooks-Gunn, J., and Waldfogel, J. "Sustained Effects of High Participation in an Early Intervention for Low-Birth-Weight Premature Infants." *Developmental Psychology,* 2003, *39*(4), 730–744.

Ialongo, N., Poduska, J., Werthamer, L., and Kellam, S. "The Distal Impact of Two First-Grade Preventive Interventions on Conduct Problems and Disorder in Early Adolescence." *Journal of Emotional and Behavioral Disorders,* 2001, *9*(3), 146–160.

Jo, B., and Muthén, B. O. "Modeling Intervention Effects with Noncompliance: A Latent Variable Approach for Randomized Trials." In G. A. Marcoulides and R. E. Schumacker (eds.), *New Developments and Techniques in Structural Equation Modeling.* Mahwah, N.J.: Erlbaum, 2001.

Leff, S. S., Power, T. J., Manz, P. H., Costigan, T. E., and Nabors, L. A. "School-Based Aggression Prevention Programs for Young Children: Current Status and Implications for Violence Prevention." *School Psychology Review,* 2001, *30*(3), 344–362.

Lochman, J. E. "Coping Power Program: Nine Month Version." Unpublished manuscript, 2003.

Lochman, J. E., Dane, H. E., Magee, T. N., Ellis, M., Pardini, D. A., and Clanton, N. R. "Disruptive Behavior Disorders: Assessment and Intervention." In B. Vance and A. Pumareiga (eds.), *The Clinical Assessment of Children and Youth Behavior: Interfacing Intervention with Assessment.* New York: Wiley, 2001.

Lochman, J. E., and Wells, K. C. "A Social-Cognitive Intervention with Aggressive Children: Prevention Effects and Contextual Implementation Issues." In R.D.V. Peters and R. J. McMahon (eds.), *Prevention of Childhood Disorders, Substance Abuse and Delinquency.* Thousand Oaks, Calif.: Sage, 1996.

Lochman, J. E., and Wells, K. C. "Contextual Social-Cognitive Mediators and Child Outcome: A Test of the Theoretical Model in the Coping Power Program." *Development and Psychopathology,* 2002a, *14*(4), 945–967.

Lochman, J. E., and Wells, K. C. "The Coping Power Program at the Middle School Transition: Universal and Indicated Prevention Effects." *Psychology of Addictive Behaviors,* 2002b, *16*(4S), S40–S54.

Lochman, J. E., and Wells, K. C. "Effectiveness of the Coping Power Program and of Classroom Intervention with Aggressive Children: Outcomes at a One-Year Follow-Up." *Behavior Therapy,* 2003, *34*(4), 493–515.

Lochman, J. E., and Wells, K. C. "The Coping Power Program for Preadolescent Boys and Their Parents: Outcome Effects at the One-Year Follow-Up." *Journal of Consulting and Clinical Psychology,* 2004, *72*(4), 571–578.

Lochman, J. E., Wells, K. C., and Murray, M. "The Coping Power Program: Preventive Intervention at the Middle School Transition." In P. Tolan, J. Szapocznik, and S. Sambrano (eds.), *Preventing Substance Abuse: 3 to 14.* Washington, D.C.: American Psychological Association, forthcoming.

Parsons, L. S. "Reducing Bias in a Propensity Score Matched-Pair Sample Using Greedy Matching Techniques." *Proceedings of the 26th Annual SAS Users Group International Conference.* Cary, N.C.: SAS Institute, 2001.

Reid, M. J., Webster-Stratton, C., and Baydar, N. "Halting the Development of Conduct Problems in Head Start Children: The Effects of Parent Training." *Journal of Clinical Child and Adolescent Psychology,* 2004, 33(2), 279–291.

Reynolds, C. R., and Kamphaus, R. W. *Behavior Assessment System for Children (BASC).* Circle Pines, Minn.: American Guidance Service, 1992.

Rubin, D. B. "Estimating Causal Effects from Large Data Sets Using Propensity Scores." *Annals of Internal Medicine,* 1997, 127(8S), 757–763.

Yau, L.H.Y., and Little, R. J. "Inference for the Complier-Average Causal Effect from Longitudinal Data Subject to Noncompliance and Missing Data, with Application to a Job Training Assessment for the Unemployed." *Journal of the American Statistical Association,* 2001, 96(456), 1232–1244.

JOHN E. LOCHMAN *is professor and Doddridge Saxon Chair in Clinical Psychology at the University of Alabama.*

CAROLINE BOXMEYER *is research scientist in the Department of Psychology at the University of Alabama.*

NICOLE POWELL *is research scientist in the Department of Psychology at the University of Alabama.*

DAVID L. ROTH *is research professor in the Department of Biostatistics at the University of Alabama at Birmingham.*

MICHAEL WINDLE *is professor of psychology and director of the Center for the Advancement of Youth at the University of Alabama at Birmingham.*

3

This chapter describes an evaluation of a teen dating violence prevention media campaign, including evaluation design and results, and the challenges that arose during the evaluation process. It makes recommendations for future evaluations of mass media campaigns that target adolescents.

Evaluation of a Teen Dating Violence Social Marketing Campaign: Lessons Learned When the Null Hypothesis Was Accepted

Emily F. Rothman, Michele R. Decker, Jay G. Silverman

Although it is somewhat disheartening to describe in detail the implementation pitfalls of a particular evaluation, the field will be enriched if we collectively pool our wisdom. This chapter discusses a three-month statewide mass media campaign to prevent teen dating violence, "See It and Stop It." The campaign reached out—using television, radio, and print advertising—and also encouraged anti-violence activism in select high schools. The objective was to drive thirteen- to seventeen-year-olds to a Web site with information about intervening with friends who might be victims or perpetrators of dating violence. To evaluate the campaign, we measured changes in ninth grade students' knowledge, attitudes, behavioral intentions, and behaviors related to dating violence in Massachusetts, where the campaign took place, and in a neighboring state, where there was no campaign exposure. The outcome was disappointing: changes in knowledge, attitudes, behavioral intentions, or behavior relative to teen dating violence did not differ for targeted students in Massachusetts and our comparison students.

How reliable were the conclusions of our evaluation study? Would it be fair to say that the campaign was not effective? The campaign and the evaluation faced several challenges that may have affected results. We

NEW DIRECTIONS FOR EVALUATION, no. 110, Summer 2006 © Wiley Periodicals, Inc.
Published online in Wiley InterScience (www.interscience.wiley.com) • DOI: 10.1002/ev.185

describe these challenges and outline several steps that might have helped to overcome them.

Background

Social marketing has been used to communicate health-related information to adults since the late 1970s (Ling, Franklin, Linsteadt, and Gearon, 1992), including promoting public awareness of hypertension (Petrella, Speechley, Kleinstiver, and Ruddy, 2005), gun safety (Meyer, Roberto, and Atkin, 2003), and emergency contraception (Trussell, Koenig, Vaughan, and Stewart, 2001). The high rate of media consumption among adolescents makes them a seemingly ideal target for social marketing via media (Brown and Witherspoon, 2002), and a handful of social marketing campaigns have been successful. These include tobacco and drug use cessation (Ishaq and Khan, 2004; Palmgreen, Donohew, Lorch, Hoyle, and Stephenson, 2001; Sly, Hopkins, Trapido, and Ray, 2001; Stephenson and others, 2002), violence prevention (Hausman, Spivak, Prothrow-Stith, and Roeber, 1992), and sexual health promotion (Kennedy and others, 2000; Mizuno, Kennedy, Weeks-Norton, and Myllyluoma, 2002). Yet mass media campaigns for youth are not always successful (Russell, Clapp, and DeJong, 2005). Many evaluations have been less than rigorous, often lacking comparison groups, consistent survey administration, or even valid and reliable survey instrumentation (Gomberg, Schneider, and DeJong, 2001). We attempted to address these limitations by including a comparison group, hiring a small number of trained graduate students for survey administration, and using valid and reliable instruments for our pre- and post-test survey.

Campaign Description

The Massachusetts Teen Action Campaign (TAC) was designed to engage teenagers in teen dating violence prevention during a three-month period in the fall of 2003 through a social diffusion or bystander approach (targeting the peers of victims or perpetrators rather than the victims or perpetrators themselves). A national advertising firm produced the campaign materials, including television, radio, and print advertisements featuring professional models and actors. The advertisements consisted of snapshots or scenarios depicting an abusive teen relationship and two checkboxes with captions that read, for example, "He hits on girls. He hits girls," or "He takes her out. He takes it out on her." The advertisements were intended to encourage teenagers to visit the campaign website and receive information about dating violence, helping abused or abusive friends, and organizing prevention projects. The campaign organizers also attempted to connect with faculty in one-third of Massachusetts high schools in order to disseminate campaign posters in these schools and recruit students to establish anti-dating violence clubs in their communities.

NEW DIRECTIONS FOR EVALUATION • DOI: 10.1002/ev

Evaluating the Campaign

We conducted pre- and post-tests with students in six Massachusetts high schools and three Connecticut high schools to evaluate the effects of the campaign. The high schools were comparable in size (roughly one thousand students each), urban or suburban location, and socio-demographics. At each of the participating schools, all ninth grade students were given the opportunity to participate in the evaluation surveys. Ninth graders were selected because they were assumed to be the least experienced in dating, have the fewest preconceptions about dating, and be most receptive to pre-vention messages. The final samples were 1,911 pre-test respondents and 1,624 post-test respondents, all ninth graders who were fifteen years old and younger.

Trained research assistants read surveys aloud to respondents during regularly scheduled classes that were required of all ninth graders (that is, English, physical education). Our survey measured teen dating violence knowledge, attitudes, behavioral intentions, demographic information (age, sex, race, ethnicity, exposure to community violence, and dating history), and knowledge of the campaign. Student exposure to the campaign was assessed with six items asking respondents to indicate the number of times in the three months prior to the survey that they had seen any TV message, radio message, billboard, poster, flyer or pamphlet, or mass transit adver-tisement about teen dating violence. We also asked respondents if they had visited any Web site specifically devoted to dating violence prevention dur-ing the three months prior to the survey, and, if so, how they found out about that Web site. Those who had visited such a Web site were prompted to write any part of the Web site address that they remembered.

Knowledge of warning signs of abuse was measured by asking students to imagine that they were dating someone and that that person engaged in particular behaviors. They were then asked to circle either "yes" or "no" to indicate if they believed each behavior was a warning sign of abuse. A sam-ple item is: "They threaten you and make you scared." Students who cor-rectly identified four or more warning signs of abuse were classified as having adequate knowledge. To measure acceptance of violence, we asked students how much they agreed with justifications for abusing partners in a variety of situations (for example, "A person flirts with someone else right in front of their date at a party"). Respondents were asked to score each item on a scale from 1–7, where 1 represented "hitting someone in this situation would not be OK," and 7 represented "hitting someone would be completely justi-fied." Students who scored any item greater than 1 were classified as having an undesirable attitude, while those who scored all items as 1 were classified as having the desired attitude. Intention to intervene with friends was measured with a series of hypothetical situations ("You are at a party and you see a guy hit his girlfriend on the arm") and eighteen possible responses ("would ignore it because it's none of my business") that students were asked to score from 1–4, where 1 represented "would never do this" and 4 represented "definitely would do this." Respondents with scores above the sample mean were classified as having a positive behavioral intention to intervene. Finally, respondents were asked if they saw or heard of peers "saying something to try to stop other kids from doing bad things to people they dated or went out with" in the previous three months. Those who responded positively were classified as having witnessed a peer intervention.

We intended to match students' pre- and post-test surveys, despite the fact that we could not collect any personal identifiers. Therefore, we used a standard self-generating unique identification code technique, which provided students with a series of five prompts to fill response boxes with letters. The prompts were: (1) the first letter of your middle name (if no middle name, put "z"), (2) the first letter of your first name, (3) the first letter of the month of your birthday, (4) the last letter of your last name, and (5) the first letter of your mother or female guardian's first name (if no female guardian, put "x"). We were unable to use the first letter of the first name, first letter of the middle name, and first letter of the last name because our Human Subjects Review committee felt that it might have been possible to determine individual student identities from their initials.

According to our post-test data, 59 percent (n = 764) of ninth grade students in Massachusetts reported seeing at least one TV, radio, billboard, or mass transit ad about dating violence or an in-school poster or a Web site, or receiving a teen dating violence community action "toolkit" during the three months of the campaign. Girls in Massachusetts were significantly more likely than boys to report having seen at least one teen dating violence media element (58 percent and 48 percent, respectively, p < .05).

According to the campaign Webmaster's count, the campaign Web site was visited by more than 32,245 unique users as many as 890,000 times during the course of the campaign. However, our survey results suggested that very few participating Massachusetts teens visited a website about teen dating violence during the campaign period (3 percent). Students who did report visiting a teen dating violence Web site following the launch of the media campaign (n = 25) were asked to name the Web site they visited. Students wrote in the names of several Web sites, but none indicated that they had visited the Web site associated with the TAC. Possible reasons for the discrepancy between the Webmaster's count and our evaluation results may be that the Web site was visited by Internet users outside of Massachusetts who discovered it through search engines, or that the Web site was visited by Massachusetts Internet users of an age group other than the one we assessed.

We detected no positive change in Massachusetts students' recognition of "warning signs of teen dating violence" from pre-test to post-test. Although there was a slight increase in the proportion of Massachusetts students who recognized what constitutes abusive behavior (that is, what "counts" as abuse) at post-test as compared to baseline (67 percent versus 73 percent, not statistically significant), the comparison students experienced a similar positive increase during the same time period (64 percent versus 70 percent, not statistically significant). Similarly, we did not detect any change in Massachusetts students' acceptance of the use of violence in relationships from baseline to post-test (57 percent versus 58 percent).

Massachusetts students were slightly more likely to report an intention to intervene with friends whom they thought were being abused or abusive at post-test as compared to baseline (42 percent versus 66 percent, p < .05), but the comparison students experienced a similar positive increase (42 percent versus 68 percent, p < .05). Massachusetts students were also no more likely to talk to friends about teen dating violence at post-test than they were at baseline (17 percent at both time points). In addition, students were actually less likely to report seeing friends intervene with potential perpetrators of dating violence at post-test than at baseline in both Massachusetts (16 percent versus 9 percent, p < .05) and Connecticut (20 percent versus 11 percent, p < .05). In sum, we were unable to conclude that the TAC campaign altered teen dating violence-related knowledge, attitudes, behavioral intentions, or behaviors.

Pitfalls of the Evaluation

A program planner might review these evaluation findings and conclude that the campaign was without success. While we would agree that there is no evidence to support the conclusion that the campaign was successful, we would like to highlight some of the challenges and "real world" difficulties that may have affected the results of our evaluation. Specifically, we would like to draw attention to (a) the influence of competing campaigns and educational programs, (b) the timing of post-test assessment, (c) our use of self-generated identifiers to track individuals across surveys, and (d) our inability to collect data from youth about personal experiences of teen dating violence victimization.

The Influence of Competing Campaigns and Educational Programs. When we embarked upon this evaluation project, we were informed by the campaign development team that teen dating violence prevention was critically under-funded and therefore a virtually ignored area of advocacy. This claim was easily verifiable at the time. In Massachusetts, state funding for teen dating violence prevention had been eliminated entirely from the state budget during the prior year, and none of the advocacy agencies in the state network of domestic violence or sexual assault programs received federal or private funds specifically to prevent teen dating violence. The national non-profit Ad Council, the most prolific producer of public service announcements in the United States, had no record of any nationally televised campaign against teen dating violence ever being conducted. We believed that the Teen Action Campaign would be breaking new ground and did not consider the possibility that similar campaigns might be launched during the same time period.

Imagine the surprise of the project research assistant who, when she first arrived at a high school in a major urban area of Connecticut (our intended "control" state) to collect data, was greeted by an enormous billboard with an explicit message about teen dating violence prevention. As it turned out, a local battered women's advocacy agency had decided to run a print media campaign to promote awareness of teen dating violence during the same time period as the Massachusetts Teen Action Campaign. To complicate matters further, a battered women's shelter near Boston, Massachusetts, launched its own teen dating violence campaign in the form of print advertising on the Boston-area subway system during the campaign period as well. These competing campaigns were problematic for our evaluation because they likely (a) attenuated differences we might otherwise have observed between Massachusetts and Connecticut respondents, and (b) boosted the observed effect of the Teen Action Campaign among Massachusetts students.

Competing media campaigns were not the only source of bias that may have influenced our results. As we learned through the course of data collection, despite state funding cuts for teen dating violence prevention, many high schools were managing to maintain some classroom education about teen dating violence through their health classes. Some schools also had special events and presentations about abuse, including inviting outside groups to perform shows or hold workshops. In short, the TAC was not students' only possible source of information about teen dating violence during the campaign period.

Historically, how have other evaluators of social marketing campaigns addressed this problem when it arose? We turn to three other published evaluation studies for our answer, including evaluations of the national "VERB" campaign to promote exercise among youth (launched by the U.S. Centers for Disease Control and Prevention in 2003), the "Kids in the Back" community-based intervention to promote rear seating for children, and the Florida "truth" anti-smoking campaign (Greenberg-Seth and others, 2004; Huhman and others, 2005; Sly, Hopkins, Trapido, and Ray, 2001). Did the evaluators of these campaigns control for competing campaigns that may have been launched by state health departments or local cities and towns during the same time period as the campaign that they were evaluating?

In all three cases, the evaluators used respondents' *self-reported recall of the campaign* as their measure of campaign exposure. For example, in the VERB campaign evaluation study, respondents were assigned to the intervention group if they recalled seeing the VERB campaign and to the control group if they had no recall of exposure to it. Respondents who recalled competing physical activity campaigns, but not the VERB campaign, were assigned to the control group. The "Kids in the Back" and Florida "truth" campaign evaluators used this same method, and Sly, Hopkins, Trapido, and Ray (2001) comment that the preferred method for determining campaign recall is to "ask a question [about recall of a campaign] that provides no advertisement-specific description but affords respondents the opportunity to offer such a description." The VERB campaign evaluation team argues that awareness of a specific media campaign is an essential first step that must occur before the desired behavior change can take place and therefore critical to assess (Huhman and others, 2005).

Because the campaign that we were evaluating was designed to change community-wide social norms and affect the culture of a school relative to dating violence, we believed that not every individual had to be directly exposed to the media elements for community-wide norms to shift. Therefore, we felt that individuals' recall of the campaign would be a less appropriate measure of exposure than the simple presence of the campaign in a given community. On the basis of this reasoning, we considered all Massachusetts adolescents "exposed" to the campaign because the state was blanketed with campaign elements. When we asked students if they had been exposed to a teen dating violence television, radio, or print ad on the survey, we did not ask them to specify the name or slogan of the advertisement.

An alternate approach would have been to ask respondents to describe the campaign they did recall or the "See It and Stop It" campaign specifically and measure changes in teen dating violence-related knowledge, attitudes, and behavior relative to their recall of that particular campaign. The benefit of this alternate approach is that we would have been able to study changes relative to recall of the particular campaign under study. The drawback would have been that some students might have experienced improvement in teen dating violence-related outcomes due to the campaign, but not have been able to recall being exposed to it because the campaign used a "social diffusion" approach (Wellings and McDowall, 2000). The campaign was designed to reach influential individuals who would disseminate key messages to peers, thereby altering the knowledge, attitudes, behavioral intentions, and behavior of the whole peer culture. It seemed reasonable to expect that positive change could occur even if only a very small proportion of students had firsthand recall of the specific campaign. Using a social diffusion theory of change, we could have missed potential effects of the campaign by assigning students without explicit recall of the campaign to the control or comparison group.

The Timing of Post-Test Assessment. The campaign was launched in October 2003 and ended on December 31, 2003. We conducted our post-test assessment in January 2004. Was conducting the post-test two weeks to one month following the end of the campaign enough time for the campaign message to "sink in" with the target audience? A longer period of time might have provided the opportunity for Massachusetts teens to digest the lessons that the campaign had to teach them, made available more time to put their new skills into practice, and yielded more dramatic improvement in the pre- to post-test scores. On the other hand, given a longer interval before post-test, students might have forgotten campaign messages over time, leading to poorer outcomes in the evaluation. What was our logic for selecting a short post-test period, and was this decision justified?

Initially, we felt that a longer period for post-test assessment (six months) would be preferable because it would have allowed us to make inferences about the longer-term effects of exposure to the campaign. However, like many evaluators, we had to balance our interest in an optimal evaluation design with the timeframe and budget constraints of our client, the campaign developer. The client expected the campaign to be a success and had a strong interest in receiving evaluation results as quickly as possible after the conclusion of the campaign so that it could be disseminated in other states. Our job was to persuade the client that the benefits of waiting for evaluation results, including a longer post-test period, would be worth the cost of the delay. Ultimately, our arguments were weighed against pressures that the client faced to deliver the campaign by a target date to a national audience. We reached a compromise about the length of the post-test period that balanced our interest in providing valid results with the client's desire for the most efficient evaluation possible.

Were there alternate ways that we might have tackled this particular challenge? One strategy that we might have tried would have been to agree to the short post-test period and also recommend an additional follow-up assessment several months later with an accompanying updated analysis. Had we made that argument, we would have had to convince the client that the financial burden of an additional assessment and the related analyses would have substantial benefits for the intervention. A realistic assessment of the budgetary constraints suggests that this argument would have been difficult. Moreover, the decision about whether or not the campaign should be adopted at the national level would likely still have been based upon the first available report, not the updated analysis.

Our Use of Self-Generated Identifiers to Track Individuals Across Surveys. Evaluation studies that involve the collection of sensitive data from adolescents (that is, abuse, dating, sexual experiences) receive special attention from human subjects committees. Collecting both sensitive and personally identifying data from adolescent subjects is particularly difficult to justify. As a result, it is usually necessary for evaluation teams to devise strategies for collecting the data of interest without collecting adolescents' names, dates of birth, social security numbers, zip codes, student identification numbers, or any other personally identifying information. How, then, can evaluators track the progress of individual participants from pre-test to post-test when an evaluation involves sensitive data?

Tracking respondents across pre- and post-tests is advantageous because it allows evaluators to control both measured and unmeasured confounds including race, personality type, or cognitive ability by examining within-person change. For this reason, we wanted to be able to self-match respondents' pre- and post-test surveys and conduct our analyses using paired samples. Because we were not permitted to collect any personally

NEW DIRECTIONS FOR EVALUATION • DOI: 10.1002/ev

identifying information for confidentiality reasons, however, we had to invent a method for prompting respondents to self-generate unique identification codes that they could write in on their surveys (described in the Methods section).

There were several problems with our code generation system that resulted in a low match rate (<20 percent). First, because our surveys were paper-and-pencil and not computer based, simply interpreting students' handwriting was a significant problem. The data entry staff was forced to guess about some of the entries and may have misread responses that were difficult to read. As well, we may have overestimated the level of skill and concentration required of students to complete the code accurately. Moreover, some of the adolescents in our sample had problems with literacy. In retrospect, the code generation instructions may have been too complicated for some, and they may have made errors while completing their codes. Also, in some cases, students may have responded to the prompts differently from one assessment to the next. For example, one prompt referred to their "mother or female guardian." Depending on individuals and their situations, it is possible that they may have referred to their biological mother during the first assessment, but their grandmother, aunt, stepmother, or foster mother on the second assessment. Finally, a substantial subset of respondents chose not to fill in their codes or did not complete them in full.

We responded to the low match rate by conducting our analyses using a snapshot method, or one that compares all respondents who took the pretest with all respondents who took the post-test, regardless of whether these two groups included exactly the same individuals. How much of an improvement would have resulted if we had instead been able to conduct an analysis of within-person change? If differences in the pre- and post-test samples were related to differences in the two samples that also predicted teen dating violence-related outcomes, our analysis did nothing to account for those possible confounds. A matched analysis would have controlled for confounds by ensuring that we were studying exactly the same set of individuals across the two sets of surveys. Because of the benefits of within-subject designs, we strongly believe that efforts to improve systems for directing respondents to generate their own unique identifiers should continue, and evaluators should broadly share their experiences with these systems.

Limitations of Our Survey Questions. While the stated objectives of the Teen Action Campaign were to create a peer climate that condemned teen dating violence in Massachusetts and to stimulate adolescent intervention with peers whom they perceived to be potential victims or perpetrators, an underlying assumption was also that the campaign would reduce actual events of teen dating violence. Ultimately, the true measure of success of any violence prevention campaign must be whether violence and its sequelae (that is, injury) are minimized.

One of the unique challenges of collecting data through schools is that representatives of the school system, which can include the superintendent, principal, or individual teachers, may have the right to determine the length of the survey and veto any questions that seem objectionable. School personnel may be weary of engaging in research projects because surveys take away from instructional time and infrequently benefit individual schools in immediate, tangible ways. Nevertheless, many schools, particularly those in communities near academic research institutions, are frequently asked to participate in national, state, and local research studies. A school will often agree to participate in a survey research project only after a review of the data collection instrument. School personnel generally err on the side of caution when deciding whether to allow potentially sensitive survey questions related to topics such as sex, drug and alcohol use, violence, or dating. From the perspective of a school administrator, the costs may outweigh the benefits of permitting researchers to ask potentially controversial questions. Most would be particularly averse to risking objections from concerned parents or community members, no matter how critically important the topic under investigation might be. As a result, many researchers and evaluators who rely upon school-based samples for behavioral health research often have to compromise the number and types of questions that they can ask, even if particular items are part of a standardized instrument or scale.

In our case, we were not permitted to pose questions about direct experiences with dating violence. Although we were allowed to ask questions about whether students talked about teen dating violence with their peers and whether they had ever witnessed a peer physically abusing a dating partner, we had no direct measure of personal teen dating violence experience. This limited our ability to make inferences about whether the campaign had an effect on the prevalence of dating violence, which arguably would have been the most meaningful information about the campaign. One solution to this problem might have been to collect data through a population-based telephone survey, but this would have been a significantly more costly option.

Conclusion and Future Directions

We faced several challenges during the implementation of our evaluation that may have compromised the validity of the study. There are several ways in which we might have improved upon our evaluation design. First, more extensive information gathering might have ensured that our comparison state would offer a true comparison (that is, no competing campaigns would take place during our data collection period). Second, we could also have included more specific questions on our survey to clarify whether respondents recalled exposure to the campaign that we were evaluating rather than other dating violence campaigns taking place during the same time period. This would have enabled us to analyze knowledge, attitude, behavioral intent, and behavior change among adolescents by their self-reported exposure to the campaign we were evaluating. Third, we could have sought supplemental funding to support an additional follow-up assessment six months after the launch of the campaign. Longer follow-up periods allow more meaningful inferences to be made about the lasting effect of the campaign as well as accommodating the potential for delayed effects of the program to emerge. Fourth, we could have designed a better system for collecting self-generated identification codes from respondents, and we might have collected data by computer (had the funding been available to do so) to improve the chances that we could match respondents across pre- and post-tests. Reliable self-matching reduces bias because it allows analyses of within-person changes. Finally, because the schools rejected questions designed to estimate the prevalence of dating violence among respondents, we could have explored alternate options for data collection outside school settings, although we might have faced similar barriers in other settings as well.

We hope that our lessons learned are useful to other evaluators who undertake assessments of social marketing campaigns. We encourage other researchers to continue to develop new methods for tracking individuals across data collection points and to explore alternate means of data collection when working within schools presents constraints that impair evaluation effectiveness. We also encourage evaluators of social marketing campaigns to always incorporate control or comparison groups into their evaluation designs. Finally, we hope that other evaluators who have the opportunity to implement evaluations of social marketing campaigns will share their experiences and results.

References

Brown, J., and Witherspoon, E. "The Mass Media and American Adolescents' Health." *Journal of Adolescent Health,* 2002, *31*(6S), 153–170.

Gomberg, L., Schneider, S. K., and DeJong, W. "Evaluation of a Social Norms Marketing Campaign to Reduce High-Risk Drinking at the University of Mississippi." *American Journal of Drug and Alcohol Abuse,* 2001, *27*(2), 375–389.

Greenberg-Seth, J., Hemenway, D., Gallagher, S. S., Ross, J. B., and Lissy, K. S. "Evaluation of a Community-Based Intervention to Promote Rear Seating for Children." *American Journal of Public Health,* 2004, *94*(6), 1009–1013.

Hausman, A., Spivak, H., Prothrow-Stith, D., and Roeber, J. "Patterns of Teen Exposure to a Community-Based Violence Prevention Project." *Journal of Adolescent Health,* 1992, *13*(8), 668–675.

Huhman, M., Potter, L. D., Wong, F. L., Banspach, S. W., Duke, J. C., and Heitzler, C. D. "Effects of a Mass Media Campaign to Increase Physical Activity Among Children: Year-1 Results of the VERB Campaign." *Pediatrics,* 2005, *116*(2), E277–E284.

Ishaq, M., and Khan, S.M.I. "The Successful Outcome of the Role of the Mass Media & School Program in the Prevention of Smoking Amongst Adolescent High School Boys." *Chest,* 2004, *126*(4), 867S.

Kennedy, M. G., Mizuno, Y., Seals, B. F., Myllyluoma, J., and Weeks-Norton, K. "Increasing Condom Use Among Adolescents with Coalition-Based Social Marketing." *Aids,* 2000, *14*(12), 1809–1818.

Ling, J., Franklin, B., Linsteadt, J., and Gearon, S. "Social Marketing: Its Place in Public Health." *Annual Review of Public Health*, 1992, *13*, 341–362.

Meyer, G., Roberto, A. J., and Atkin, C. K. "A Radio-Based Approach to Promoting Gun Safety: Process and Outcome Evaluation Implications and Insights." *Health Communication*, 2003, *15*(3), 299–318.

Mizuno, Y., Kennedy, M., Weeks-Norton, K., and Myllyluoma, J. "An Examination of Adolescents Who Were and Were Not Exposed to 'Teens Stopping AIDS': Reaching the Hard-to-Reach." *Journal of Health Communication*, 2002, *7*(3), 197–203.

Palmgreen, P., Donohew, L., Lorch, E. P., Hoyle, R. H., and Stephenson, M. T. "Television Campaigns and Adolescent Marijuana Use: Tests of Sensation Seeking Targeting." *American Journal of Public Health*, 2001, *91*(2), 292–296.

Petrella, R. J., Speechley, M., Kleinstiver, P. W., and Ruddy, T. "Impact of a Social Marketing Media Campaign on Public Awareness of Hypertension." *American Journal of Hypertension*, 2005, *18*(2), 270–275.

Russell, C. A., Clapp, J. D., and DeJong, W. "Done 4: Analysis of a Failed Social Norms Marketing Campaign." *Health Communication*, 2005, *17*(1), 57–65.

Sly, D., Hopkins, R., Trapido, E., and Ray, S. "Influence of a Counteradvertising Media Campaign on Initiation of Smoking: The Florida 'Truth' Campaign." *American Journal of Public Health*, 2001, *91*(2), 233–238.

Stephenson, M., Morgan, S., Lorch, E., Palmgreen, P., Donohew, L., and Hoyle, R. "Predictors of Exposure from an Antimarijuana Media Campaign: Outcome Research Assessing Sensation Seeking Targeting." *Health Communication*, 2002, *14*(1), 23–43.

Trussell, J., Koenig, J., Vaughan, B., and Stewart, F. "Evaluation of a Media Campaign to Increase Knowledge About Emergency Contraception." *Contraception*, 2001, *63*(2), 81–87.

Wellings, K., and McDowall, W. "Evaluating Mass Media Approaches to Health Promotion: A Review of Methods." *Health Education*, 2000, *100*, 23–32.

EMILY F. ROTHMAN *is assistant professor of social and behavioral sciences at the Boston University School of Public Health.*

MICHELE R. DECKER *is a doctoral student of society, human development, and health at the Harvard School of Public Health.*

JAY G. SILVERMAN *is assistant professor of society, human development and health at the Harvard School of Public Health.*

NEW DIRECTIONS FOR EVALUATION • DOI: 10.1002/ev

4

This chapter focuses on lessons concerning the design of interventions and the interpretation of outcome and cost-benefit analyses. An intervention can "fail" due to the implementation of an intervention component in the context of standard treatments, and the interpretation of costs and benefits can change substantially if one considers the alternative long-term outcomes in the absence of the intervention.

How Much of a Good Thing Is Too Much? Explaining the Failure of a Well-Designed, Well-Executed Intervention in Juvenile Hall for "Hard-to-Place" Delinquents

Robert Nash Parker, Emily K. Asencio, Deborah Plechner

This is a report of an unsuccessful evaluation of a program for "hard-to-place" juvenile offenders in a California county. The program was well designed and reasonably well executed, with problems of implementation and fidelity that are quite typical of field interventions. Yet as the analysis that follows demonstrates, every hypothesis proposed from the outset was rejected.

Although the decade of the 1990s witnessed a decline in adult crime and violence rates in California and the United States in general, juvenile crime and violence remained a significant problem. In California, juvenile assault arrests remained at 12.5 per one hundred thousand between 1994 and 1999; adult arrest rates for the same crime declined nearly 12 percent (California Attorney General's Office, 2004). In San Bernardino County, where our project took place, juvenile murder arrest rates more than

---

Note: The authors would like to thank the Juvenile Probation Department, County of San Bernardino, California, including Don Brotchie, Ron Cutler, William Stevenson, George Post, and Ernie Engeron. Funding came from the California State Board of Corrections. The content remains the responsibility of the authors.

doubled in 2000, from five per one hundred thousand youth to nearly eleven per one hundred thousand.

In response to the seeming intractability of juvenile offending, the California Juvenile Justice system engaged in a get-tough campaign, which resulted in a 30 percent increase in the caseload of the county juvenile justice system (San Bernardino County Department of Probation, 1999). The main Juvenile Hall in San Bernardino City has a rated capacity of 240 but had a population in late 1999 of more than 500: tents were set up in the parking lot to hold the overflow of incarcerated youth (Nelson, 2001). The county also faced an increase in sentences for juvenile offenders involving out-of-home placements. Youthful offenders with consistently escalating patterns of offending were thought to benefit from a secure placement away from home and community influences and one that also offered rehabilitation services such as moral guidance, behavioral therapy, psychiatric treatment, and vocational training. In San Bernardino County, these placements increased from 306 in 1996 to more than 600 in 1998. A number of youth were placed out-of-state at great expense; in 1998 the state restricted such placements to reduce costs, resulting in an even bigger demand for local placements.

The county also saw an increase in hard-to-place offenders; by 1998, 17 percent of out-of-home placements were hard-to-place youth. It took almost twice as long to place such youth compared to the general offender population, significantly increasing costs, so that each hard-to-place offender added nearly $8,000 to the costs of Juvenile Hall.

Program Description

The Placement Readiness and Evaluation Program, or PREP, was designed to address difficulties with hard-to-place youth. Private placements were reluctant to take such youth into their facilities because certain characteristics, such as defiant personalities, assaultive behavior, suicide ideation, bed wetting, alcohol and drug addiction, fire setting, and running away, made them more difficult to manage.

PREP was designed to address this population by removing youth from Juvenile Hall. PREP resembled a residential placement facility, and, in PREP, youth would be prepared for the routine of a placement facility. The "hard-to-place" label was not understood by the private placement operators. A checklist item may suggest that an offender is "hard to place" due to a defiant personality, but a current psychiatric assessment might reveal no such condition. The "hard-to-place" label may have resulted from characteristics of a prior placement that would not apply in the new placement. Youthful offenders may mature out of some problems, such as bed wetting. Thus the stabilized, readied, and more completely assessed youthful offender would achieve a faster placement, reduce placement failures, and significantly reduce county costs.

New Directions for Evaluation • DOI: 10.1002/ev

Implementation Issues

The PREP project suffered from implementation issues. Although existing space was remodeled, the remodeling resembled a new construction project to create space with four or five residential rooms for sleeping and hanging out, built for two or three youth comfortably, with a total capacity of thirteen. A full-time director supervised two line supervisors and six probation correctional officers. Staff also included a full-time teacher and a full-time licensed therapist who were responsible for up to thirteen youth during the day. At night, three night supervisors were on duty between 10 P.M. and 6 A.M.

Significant turnover in the staff, beginning with the retirement of the architect and designated director of the unit shortly after funding was awarded, resulted in difficulties. Subsequent managers did their best, but a program like PREP is often successful because of the vision of founders. Significant unit staff turnover contributed to a sense of instability. Some believed in the treatment approach embodied in PREP's design, while others saw the unit as a form of punishment for bad behavior. This difference sometimes detracted from efforts to follow the PREP mandate of treatment, evaluation, and readiness.

Construction delayed the PREP unit opening by seven months. Once the unit began to function, operational problems came to light. First, there were difficulties in identifying "hard-to-place" youth. Initially, probation officers who supervised youth placements and filled out screening checklists specified every single characteristic as being true for every youth; this practice led to universal eligibility. Subsequently, PREP established more comprehensive assessments and more stringent criteria and too few youth were identified. After adjusting the number of criteria, a compromise was reached. However, no evidence came to light in the evaluation to suggest that these selection problems seriously disrupted the project.

Another implementation issue was pressure to keep PREP full. PREP represented an increase in the capacity of Juvenile Hall, even though it had only thirteen beds. A vacancy in the unit in some cases was filled by a youth who had already failed in the PREP unit or had been placed and suffered a placement failure. Bringing these youth back into the PREP unit may have contaminated the design and the atmosphere of the unit, but an investigation revealed fewer than ten cases during the study. As well, the overall structure of the unit created difficulties. Housing both males and females (who represented only 17 percent of the youth) together created behavior problems. In addition, the wide age range (eleven to seventeen) and the disparity in experience and offending history between PREP residents who had previously been sentenced to Juvenile Hall and first-time residents all added to the complex interpersonal dynamics.

NEW DIRECTIONS FOR EVALUATION • DOI: 10.1002/ev

Finally, there was a lack of cooperation from outside agencies. The placement probation officers were instructed to look for potential matches between PREP youth and placement facilities in their territories, but officers outside the City of San Bernardino ignored PREP. Those assigned to the city dealt with caseloads that were so large as to preclude careful assessment of potential placement options, and they were thus less than willing to participate in the more complex procedures necessary to refer youth to the PREP experimental intervention. Aftercare probation officers were equally unwilling or unable to cooperate and coordinate with the PREP team; as a result, aftercare was probably the least well-implemented part of PREP. Most importantly, operators of outside placement facilities frequently ignored PREP and the additional assessments and evaluations that were available for youth on the unit. The county seemed to have little control over the placements, despite the fact that these organizations collected on average $5,000 per month for each youth housed.

Problematic Developments: External Shocks and Internal Changes

As PREP was beginning to operate, changing circumstances at state and local levels simultaneously began to undermine the fundamental premises of the project. These trends diluted the justification of PREP as an approach for hard-to-place detainees and changed the way in which sentences for such youth were constructed. The result of several important trends led to significant changes in the operation of the juvenile court and juvenile correctional systems.

First, the deepening budget crisis of the State of California caused the State to rethink the entire initiative. The dot-com boom of the mid-1990s that produced a windfall for the state had also supported experimentation in public policy. However, with the dot-com bust in the late 1990s, the state entered an increasingly precarious financial position. With two years completed for the experimental program that was initially funded for three years and subsequently extended to four years, the state legislature made a substantial budget cut, ending all projects, including PREP. PREP ceased operations after two years and five months. Evaluation research and follow-up data collection processes continued for another twelve months, but the program was ended about two years before the end date anticipated in the original evaluation design.

The financial pressures from the state, the costs to the county for out-of-home placements, and the organizational difficulties of the PREP unit combined with the continued pressure to reduce general overcrowding at Juvenile Hall also resulted in a significant decline in new offenders eligible for PREP. For example, the juvenile court began to implement newer sentencing techniques such as electronic home monitoring, and these strategies reduced the number of eligible detainees and made recruiting more difficult.

NEW DIRECTIONS FOR EVALUATION • DOI: 10.1002/ev

Overall, these changing circumstances in both Sacramento and San Bernardino resulted in undermining the rationale for PREP. Those managing the unit had difficulty maintaining the argument that PREP had a special function and should only serve a certain population; other managers in Juvenile Hall saw PREP as just another unit with potential space to relieve overcrowding. However, both the program staff and managers of PREP and the state funding agency still had hopes that an outcome evaluation would support the notion that PREP was based on sound principles. A successful evaluation would set the stage for a renewed interest in this type of program when the state's fortunes revived.

Evaluation Design Issues

The PREP evaluation was a randomized experimental trial. Intake probation officers were to assess youth incoming to Juvenile Hall with a standardized instrument to determine whether they were hard to place. If a youth was classified, his or her name was faxed to the evaluation team, and an attempt would be made to interview the youth for participation and informed consent. If the youth agreed to participate, he or she was randomly assigned to PREP or to the control group residing in Juvenile Hall. If space was available in the PREP unit, the youth was transferred; if not, he or she remained in Juvenile Hall on a waiting list. Between March 2000 and August 2002, 447 participants were successfully recruited from a total of 663 classified as hard to place; 35 youth declined participation. Some youth were placed before they could be assigned to PREP even after selection and informed consent; some youth were placed before a consent interview could be arranged. Such sample selection bias had an unknown impact.

Initial Evaluation Findings

Our findings are based on two sources: quantitative outcome data and an in-depth interview sample of twenty youth who entered PREP between December 13, 2001, and April 1, 2002. The youth we interviewed were eighteen males and two females, aged thirteen to eighteen. Nearly half (nine) were Caucasian, with one-quarter (five) Hispanic and one-quarter (five) African American; one was Asian American. Half of these youth resided with only their mothers prior to coming into Juvenile Hall, and eight came from two-parent households. The remaining youth were in various institutional settings prior to entering Juvenile Hall.

Our qualitative data make clear that youth preferred the PREP unit to the other units that they had lived in at Juvenile Hall. Longer, hot showers taken in privacy were one benefit of PREP; others included carpeted floors, tables and chairs in the common living area, and hot food. Several youth mentioned that having a roommate prevented the feelings of isolation that they experienced in Juvenile Hall. One young man said he liked having a roommate because "you don't go crazy like sitting around talking to yourself, making faces out of bricks, counting the bricks in the room like I was doing." Having a roommate meant these youth were not isolated even when restricted to their rooms. Two other features of PREP also helped counter boredom and isolation: more free time and more activities during free time. Many of these activities were integrated into learning experiences in the unit's classroom.

The youths' comments also reflected their shared perception that staff treated them differently in PREP. Several youth said that the staff members working in PREP were nicer, listened, helped or worked with them more, were more lenient, and spent more time talking with them about their lives. The ratio of youth to staff members was much lower in PREP, reducing both the levels of real and potential conflict among youth and the amount of time that staff spent interacting with each youth. As one young woman put it, "I like the PREP unit because instead of yelling at you, they work with you. They show you love."

There were a few youth who claimed to dislike PREP. One young man who had conflicts with staff and youth elsewhere had similar problems in PREP. He also had difficulties getting along with the teacher; he claimed the teacher disliked him. He also said that staff did not like him and that there were "too many staff." As he put it: "I get more hours here than I used to. I've been in trouble since I came here." For this young man and another who also disliked PREP, being in the unit was difficult because of its size and remoteness from the rest of Juvenile Hall. Both young men said they missed being able to mingle with other youth in the dining hall or the tents. They claimed that Juvenile Hall was more "fun" because they could socialize with a larger group. However, these comments were unusual. In general, the youth found life in PREP far superior to their prior experiences elsewhere.

Although PREP had several components that were supposed to affect placement, it was the physical experience of being in the PREP unit that was most noticeable to the youth. Four-fifths of the interview sample commented on how they thought that being in PREP might or might not help them to succeed in placement. Eleven of them said that they thought that being in PREP would help them to do better in placement because it was "like placement."

The two youth who had been in placement before mentioned different aspects of the program as positive influences: therapy, dealing with a roommate, and the difference in the level of structure found in PREP. One young woman's statement exemplifies the youths' views on the level of structure in PREP and how that might help prepare for placement: "When I was in Juvenile Hall and I went to placement, it was a real quick, sudden move. You're used to being locked up in your little cell, you're used to walking with your hands behind your back, and so when you get to placement they show you love. . . . Here they are showing you love and so when you get to placement, you're not going to still walk with your hands behind your back. You'll just be more ready physically and emotionally."

It seems clear that PREP created a truly different experience for these youth. PREP in this sense was successful beyond all expectations. Compared to all the other places in the system these youth had been or would go, PREP was clearly preferred, so much so that even youth who had been in PREP, gone to placement, been released from placement, and had re-offended wanted to go back to PREP. Yet it was this very success that placed the PREP unit in jeopardy of failure as an alternative treatment for hard-to-place offenders.

Quantitative Contrasts and Their Meaning

Our quantitative evaluation included 447 youth: 260 in PREP and 187 in the control group. We evaluated their progress at three follow-up periods after the youth had left the placement: six months, twelve months, and eighteen months.

Four basic outcomes were established for PREP, and these guided the outcome evaluation. The four hypotheses that flowed from expected outcomes were:

H1: Following program separation, program participants will have fewer arrests than juveniles who have received standard probation treatment.
H2: Program participants will spend fewer days, on average, awaiting placement in Juvenile Hall than non-program participants.
H3: Program participants will spend fewer days, on average, in placement than non-program participants.
H4: Program participants will be less likely than non-program participants to experience placement failure.

To test the first hypothesis, we tracked the number of new arrests in each of the three follow-up periods, starting with the exit of each participant, PREP or control, from his or her out-of-home placement. As the number of multiple arrests was small, this measure was coded 1 if a participant had 1 or more arrests in the period. The number of days in each period, either time to arrest or six months if no arrest, was recorded so that the rate of new arrests could be calculated and analyzed. As most youth did not have an arrest and are thus censored, we used survival analysis, a technique that assesses the impact of covariates on the rate at which individuals move from one state of being to another, taking account of the time to the transition as well as the likelihood of a transition itself, to analyze these transition rates. In other words, what is the rate at which members of the two groups leave PREP and enter a placement—is that rate slower or faster for the PREP treatment group, and what factors or characteristics influence this rate of transition? For the second hypothesis, we calculated the number of days youth in both groups spent from their entry into Juvenile Hall, including the time in PREP, until they were placed. Third, we measured the number of days both groups spent in out-of-home placements after leaving PREP or Juvenile Hall. Finally, placement failures were measured, that is, cases in which youth ran away or were rejected by the placement for some other reason after being assigned.

Independent variables used in the multivariate analyses were demographic characteristics including gender, ethnicity (African Americans and Latinos), and age. Indicators of hard-to-place status, including past assaultive behavior, a defiant attitude, a drug problem, an alcohol problem, and a prior gang affiliation were included as well. Also included were a set of measures concerning prior experience with the justice system: prior arrests (total), prior placements (total), prior evidence of abuse or neglect including sexual abuse, prior mental illness, and prior experience with psychotropic prescription medication. We also included an indicator of educational status, coded 1 if the youth was below grade level, and a measure of disability, physical, or psychological. We included an indicator of current medication and, finally, an indicator of current marijuana use.

In examining the rate of new arrests for our participants, no effects of PREP were statistically significant. The only factors that were statistically significant for new arrests at first follow-up were prior arrests and ethnicity. We used survival analysis to investigate the rate at which subjects were re-arrested after placement. We reasoned that, even if the overall rate was the same, PREP might have had the effect of slowing down the rate of new arrests. However, participation in the PREP treatment group had no impact. Indeed, none of the variables had an impact on the time to arrest. The second follow-up period showed the same results: no statistically significant difference between PREP and control groups in new arrests. The only significant predictor was prior number of arrests. Similarly, survival analysis of the rate of new arrests in the second follow-up period shows no significant effects. At the third follow-up assessment, only two factors were significant predictors: being below grade level and current marijuana use. Survival analysis also revealed that the rate of new arrests was increased by current marijuana use and being below grade level.

When we examined time to placement, the average wait was forty-nine days for PREP youth and fifty-one days for controls. Although this is down for both groups from the period before the county initiated the PREP intervention, again we found little or no difference between the two groups. However, four net effects were statistically significant in predicting time to arrest: assaultive personality ($F = 4.93$), prior placements ($F = 10.91$), prior arrests ($F = 31.32$), and current marijuana use ($F = 10.05$). The survival analysis for the rate to placement also showed an overall significant impact of these four predictors, as well as two additional characteristics. Six measures all significantly lengthened the time before these youth were placed: an assaultive personality, prior arrests, current marijuana use, past psychotropic medicine experience, being a victim of past sexual abuse, and having had a prior mental illness.

Results of our analysis of time spent in placement showed that PREP youth spent about ten days longer in placement, but the difference was not statistically significant. The survival analysis revealed that the only variable to affect the time in placement was a prior alcohol problem, and the impact of this variable was to speed up the youth's exit from placement. Again, there was little or no support for our expectation that PREP youth would spend a shorter amount of time in placement. Finally, PREP youth were actually more likely to show placement failure, although, again, this difference was not statistically significant.

Interpreting the Contrasts: When Is Failure a Success?

It seems clear from our qualitative data that the PREP experience for the participating youth was dramatically different from conditions that they experienced in either traditional Juvenile Hall settings or alternative placement settings. Indeed, the program gave them some benefits that were not available to them in their own neighborhoods or even in their families. Therefore, when the youth were forced to leave PREP and enter a placement setting, our data suggest they did everything they could to have another chance at PREP. The fastest way to gain access to PREP was to fail at the placement. Going AWOL, being expelled from a placement, or even committing another crime once released from what was considered to be a successful placement, all of which the treatment group did at higher rates than the control group, constituted a path back for these youth into Juvenile Hall, where they would ask and plead to be sent back to PREP.

The design of the intervention, of course, as well as the intent of the evaluation prohibited reentry by previous participants. Youth who participated after multiple failures could contaminate possible effects of the experimental PREP treatment. However, after the program was ended, we conducted process evaluation interviews and focus group interviews with staff. These interviews revealed that some youth had been readmitted to the PREP unit. Our qualitative evidence suggested that this happened in fewer than ten cases over the two and-one-half-year life of PREP. Further, these new cases were not included in the final data set that we submitted to the state, nor were they used as a part of the outcome evaluation. The staff readily admitted that they knew this kind of a readmit was a violation of the study protocol. As a result, they hid the presence of these youth whom they were willing to readmit and simply neglected to file the regular data reports that were filed on all of the "recognized" PREP participants.

It is not at all clear that every youth who was readmitted to PREP represented a potentially significant source of contamination for the evaluation. Many of the youth who were appropriately assigned to PREP in the study came in with previous experience in the placement system. Thus, any unique contamination, or contamination from causes other than prior history with juvenile justice, would have come only from the PREP youth who had actually made it into the unit prior to placement, subsequently failed at their placement, and were recycled directly back into the unit without any time of separation from custody. The immediacy of their recent experience in the PREP experimental unit might have had an unmeasured and therefore unknown influence on participants who were coming into PREP for the first time at the same time that recycled participants were reentering. These reentry youth might also have contaminated the study by biasing the sample in unknown ways because they were filling beds in PREP that could have been allocated to new youth coming into the system and coming to PREP for the first time. However, by the end of the evaluation study period, the availability of those who fit the evaluation protocol had dropped significantly, and the press to fill the beds with youth might have resulted in those recycled youth being reassigned to PREP in any case.

The desire of these youth to be reinstated in the PREP unit does provide support for the notion that the PREP unit was a victim of its own success in providing a positive, emotionally supportive environment for these youthful offenders. The rate at which the treatment group failed at placement, for example, was apparently influenced by the contrast between the positive environment that was provided at PREP and the difficulties that came with being a part of the general population in Juvenile Hall, assignment to an out-of-home placement facility, rejoining a dysfunctional family, or being released back onto the streets in the decaying neighborhoods from which many of these youth came.

The Costs and Benefits of Success and Failure: Lessons Learned from the PREP Evaluation

The overall costs for the PREP project were $4,532,465, including an administrative overhead charge of $782,379 and $343,863 to conduct the evaluation research. Of that amount, the Bureau of Corrections provided $2,588,531, and the County provided matching funds in the amount of $1,142,613. Given that our participants in the control condition did not receive any direct benefits from the PREP project, calculating the cost per youth would require dividing $4,532,465 by 240 PREP participants. The resulting per youth cost of $18,885 for three years represents $6,295 per youth per year. This calculation also ignores the additional expenses incurred by all incarcerated youth for their stay in Juvenile Hall, their court costs, placements costs, and the supervision costs that commence after the youth are released. Given that there is no evidence that suggests PREP reduced recidivism, prevented placement failures, reduced time to placement, or reduced time in placement, there is no means to adequately calculate benefits or savings from PREP. Therefore, the standard cost-benefit model suggests the PREP experiment was cost ineffective. It added substantial costs per youth in each year of operation, and there is no evidence of any cost savings to the larger society or the juvenile justice system as a result of the program. However, if we make a more nuanced examination of the overall findings, we arrive at a much different conclusion.

We have argued that PREP failed in part because it was too much of a good thing, compared to alternative environments for youthful detainees. Therefore one conclusion to be drawn is that when working with program developers to design an intervention, evaluators should be thoroughly familiar with the nature of the intervention in comparison to the control or standard treatment condition. If a behavior-change treatment is so attractive that participants maintain a behavior in order to remain in treatment, evaluation outcomes may be influenced in an unexpected manner. The classic role of the "outside" evaluator, called in after the establishment of an intervention program, is not sustainable in such a case. The evaluation team should be involved from the start of the project to be sure that the design of the evaluation complements the intervention. The goal of early involvement is to insure that the evaluation accurately captures the contrast between the "business as usual" treatment and a very different treatment condition. The extreme contrasts between Juvenile Hall placement and PREP placement contributed to an apparent failure of PREP according to the quantitative evaluation data. However, additional assessments might have more adequately captured the attractive quality of the PREP unit and helped explain the paradoxical findings. For example, important outcome indicators for the PREP evaluation might have included such measures as disciplinary incidents in custody or educational progress prior to placement. Traditional outcome measures usually investigated in a particular substantive area may not always be the best ones when there is such a powerful and attractive contrast between treatment and control conditions.

The interpretation of a cost-benefit calculation provides a final lesson for this evaluation. Although the data for this project show no benefits or cost savings, a more important calculation in this instance would contrast the costs of the current intervention against likely outcomes that might have resulted in the absence of the intervention. The cost data show that $6,300 was spent keeping 242 youth in PREP for an average of forty-nine days, or about $129 per day per youth. Thus to keep 650 youth (an estimate of the entire Juvenile Hall population in San Bernardino during these years) for 365 days in a PREP-like unit would cost approximately $30,605,250, or about $51,000 per year per youth. However, if a juvenile facility based on the PREP model were to prevent half of these youth from going on to adult criminal careers, the ultimate cost savings could be considerable. The costs of adult imprisonment for twenty-five years (the typical sentence of the "three strikes" program in California) with prisoner per year costs estimated at about $38,000 (California Department of Corrections and Rehabilitation Budget, 2005–2006) reach approximately $950,000 per prisoner. Thus PREP represents the potential for a total savings of more than $300 million from just one county. These figures make the costs for PREP-like units seem reasonable. Another useful comparison is to look at the cost of imprisoning a youth in what used to be known as the California Youth Authority, estimated to be over $80,000 per youth per year (California Department of Corrections and Rehabilitation Budget, 2005–2006). If PREP-like units could prevent one hundred commitments per year to this alternative, cost savings would be enough to pay for 166 PREP resident youth for a year from just one county. Again, in this example, the costs of intervention are quite reasonable compared to the costs of business as usual for juvenile justice. In sum, the additional cost of the PREP unit turns out to be rather small in comparison to the enormous costs of imprisoning the failures of the juvenile detention system in California. So the larger policy lesson is that effective reform of the juvenile justice system may require a radically different mind set about the goals of detention, a mind set that can understand the evidence from this "failed" evaluation as an indicator of the kind of treatment that would be truly effective and desirable for the future of youth caught up in the juvenile justice system.

Perhaps an alternative conclusion would be that PREP is just a bad idea. If so, this "bad idea" is at the spearhead of juvenile justice and correlational reform in the United States and Canada. For example, in Missouri, juvenile corrections was completely reformed beginning in the 1980s—the state closed all of its penitentiary-style youth facilities, distributed small facilities based on a cottage model similar to the PREP project, many with a twelve-youth capacity, backed by intensive staff involvement and a twenty-four-hour-a-day therapy model that focuses on treatment, education, and rehabilitation. Studies of recidivism indicate that 75 percent of the youth who have left such facilities have no criminal justice involvement after three years (Mendel, 2000). In Canada, after a serious prison riot was filmed in the national Women's Prison in Kingston, Ontario, and the film was widely distributed in government and press circles, a reform movement was initiated that resulted in the closing of the prison in Kingston and the construction of five new regional facilities fashioned along the same lines as the PREP unit. In one case, an indigenous people's model was used to construct a healing lodge. In the four facilities dealing with a largely Anglo-Canadian population, housing units were constructed as small cottages, with ten to twelve inmates and five to eight staff members in each cottage. The programs and interventions were inmate specific and intensive, similar to the PREP model, and the idea was to prepare and stabilize these inmates for release back into society. Education and job skills are stressed in the programming in these facilities (Hayman, 2000). These experiences and others suggest that PREP-style juvenile corrections is the future of reform, and that may be the most important lesson learned from this failed evaluation.

References

California Attorney General's Office. *Crime in California.* Sacramento, Calif.: California Criminal Justice Statistics Center, 2004.

California Department of Corrections and Rehabilitation. 2006. "Budget Overview." http://www.corr.ca.gov/BudgetRegs/budgetOverview.html.

Hayman, S. "Prison Reform and Incorporation: Lessons from Britain and Canada." In M. Shaw and K. Hannah-Moffat (eds.), *An Ideal Prison? Critical Essays on Women's Imprisonment in Canada.* Halifax: Fernwood Publishing, 2000.

Mendel, R. A. "Less Costs, More Safety: Guiding Lights for Reform in Juvenile Justice." Washington, D.C.: American Youth Policy Forum, 2000.

Nelson, J. "Tents Pitched as a Solution to Crowding." *San Bernardino Sun,* Nov. 29, 2001, Local Section.

San Bernardino Probation Department. "PREP Project: Challenge Grant II Proposal to the California Board of Corrections." Unpublished manuscript.

ROBERT NASH PARKER is professor of sociology and director of the Presley Center for Crime and Justice Studies at the University of California, Riverside.

EMILY K. ASENCIO is a postdoctoral scholar at the Academic Center for Excellence on Youth Violence Prevention at the University of California, Riverside.

DEBORAH PLECHNER is assistant professor of sociology and criminology in the Sociology-Anthropology Department at the University of Minnesota, Duluth.

5

Over the past decades, public concern over youth violence has led to a proliferation of prevention programs as well as a corresponding push to identify programs that "work." A more accurate understanding of effectiveness as well as failure can be found by reframing the questions to ask what works, for whom, and under what conditions.

What Works (and What Does Not) in Youth Violence Prevention: Rethinking the Questions and Finding New Answers

Nancy G. Guerra, Paul Boxer, Clayton R. Cook

Dramatic rises in youth violence in the United States beginning in the 1980s coupled with high visibility acts such as school shootings have resulted in a corresponding proliferation of programs designed to prevent aggression and violence in children and youth. Parallel with this increasing programmatic expansion, there have been repeated calls for rigorous evaluations of programs and identification of "best practices" that merit dissemination and implementation.

Still, in spite of extensive efforts to document effective practices in youth violence prevention, there remains a somewhat confusing array of evidence for effectiveness and lack of effectiveness, as well as a broad range of interpretations of this evidence.

On the one hand, there are clear indications that individual programs can have an impact on preventing or reducing aggression and related behaviors, and positive evaluations of specific programs abound (Farrell, Meyer, and White, 2001; Henggeler and others, 1996). Looking at program reviews and meta-analysis, positive effects have been evident primarily with certain types of programs—most typically those derived from cognitive-behavioral principles (Guerra, Boxer, and Kim, forthcoming; Wilson, Lipsey, and Derzon, 2003). On the other hand, some reviews of program outcomes and attempts to

NEW DIRECTIONS FOR EVALUATION, no. 110, Summer 2006 © Wiley Periodicals, Inc.
Published online in Wiley InterScience (www.interscience.wiley.com) • DOI: 10.1002/ev.187

identify model programs have been less encouraging. For instance, a recent conference convened by the National Institute of Health (NIH) attempted to find a consensus on prevention programs for adolescents based on a commissioned meta-analysis of studies since 1995 (Chan and others, 2004). Only sixty-seven of more than sixteen hundred studies of youth violence prevention programs were included on the basis of rigorous scientific criteria, and evidence for effectiveness was noted in only fourteen studies. Similarly, a center at the University of Colorado has been reviewing youth violence prevention programs to designate "blueprint" programs based on rigorous standards in evaluation and the existence of at least one replication; only eleven programs out of hundreds examined have been selected as blueprint interventions (Mihalic and others, 2004).

From both a program and a policy perspective, it is at best difficult to sift through this seemingly contradictory assortment of evidence. Perhaps the key to unlocking this array of findings and interpretations is to rethink the very questions addressed. Asking "what works" in youth violence prevention suggests a simple, dichotomous answer (that is, works or does not work) about efforts to prevent or modify a problem behavior marked by its complexity and the multiplicity of associated risk and protective mechanisms (Boxer and Dubow, 2002; Cicchetti and Rogosch, 1996; Guerra and Huesmann, 2004). Even under the best circumstances it is unlikely that a violence prevention program "worked" for all: some participants may have improved, some may have stayed the same, and some may have increased their aggression, as has been noted in recent examinations of iatrogenic or negative effects interventions (Boxer, Guerra, Huesmann, and Morales, 2005; Dishion, McCord, and Poulin, 1999).

In the present chapter, we suggest that a more accurate understanding of effectiveness as well as failure can be found by reframing the questions and corresponding evaluation designs. Rather than asking, "What works in youth violence prevention?" we suggest that it is most important to ask: (a) what works and what does not work, (b) for whom, and (c) under what conditions? We discuss each component in more detail, providing illustrative examples from a large-scale prevention study, the Metropolitan Area Child Study (MACS). As we point out, this study provides an example of a multi-component, multi-context intervention that was more effective for some children and less effective for others.

Of course, the importance of assessing effectiveness for moderators of intervention is by no means a recent phenomenon, as several researchers have advocated for this type of investigation for quite some time (Frick, 2001; Kazdin, 2002). Such research has been seen as critical for providing valuable information that will lend itself to a better "fit" between the individual and the intervention. However, despite the recognized importance of examining moderators, it is also the case that beyond considerations of age and sex differences in outcomes, relatively few studies of youth violence prevention programs systematically address potential moderators of outcomes. As we discuss in this chapter, an important next step is to define more carefully characteristics of individuals and contexts that can maximize program fit.

The Metropolitan Area Child Study (MACS)

MACS was a longitudinal, quasi-experimental aggression prevention field study that included eight cohorts of urban and inner-city elementary school children (Metropolitan Area Child Study Research Group, 2002). Because of the multiply determined nature of children's aggression, particularly in more disadvantaged urban settings characterized by high rates of crime and poverty and sparse availability of community resources, a central hypothesis of the study was that interventions under these more difficult circumstances needed to be multi-year and multi-component, and target cognition, skills, and behavior across multiple contexts. At the same time, limited funding for comprehensive prevention programming, even when found effective, may preclude adequate funding of such programs, particularly in poorer communities. To address both concerns, we designed the study to test multiple levels of intervention effort over a two-year period that involved individual children as well as teachers and classrooms, the peer group, and the family. The design included four experimental conditions, with each condition representing an increase in dosage and extension of contexts affected. Specifically, schools were randomly assigned to one of four conditions: level A, classroom-only general enhancement program (two-year social-cognitive curriculum and teacher training); level B, classroom enhancement plus small group intervention for high-risk children (two-year intensive social-cognitive training); level C, classroom enhancement plus small group plus family intervention for high-risk children (one-year family therapy); and level D, no treatment control.

We also were interested in examining moderators of intervention effectiveness at the individual and school or community level. At the individual level, we addressed the question of whether developmental timing within the elementary school years would affect intervention outcomes. Given the trend toward "earlier is better" in the field of prevention research and practice, we wanted to examine empirically whether outcomes varied for children who began the program in the early (Grades 2–3) versus late (Grades 5–6) elementary school years.

At the school or community level, many studies have reported that preventive interventions do not work equally well in all settings, with economic and social constraints often limiting the ability of interventions to effect change in aggression (Aber and others, 2002; Hughes and others, 2005). To test whether school or community resources moderated intervention outcomes, schools in our study were divided into low-resource schools and moderate-resource schools based on a broad array of school and community indicators, including neighborhood crime and violence rates, funding allocations, number of children receiving free or reduced lunch, and number of rental housing units.

As we have reported previously, the intervention was effective in preventing aggression in some but not all children. A more complete description of the study design, interventions, and results can be found in the report of the Metropolitan Area Child Study Research Group (MACS) (2002). In some cases, iatrogenic effects were noted. As we will discuss in more detail in the following sections, effects on aggression were moderated by individual and school or community factors. Had we not examined these moderators and looked only at main effects across all children and schools, we would have concluded that the intervention did not work. However, a more accurate conclusion was that the intervention worked for some children under some conditions and did not work for other children under other conditions.

Rethinking the Question: What Works and What Does Not Work

The long-term goal of the MACS intervention was to prevent serious violent behavior among urban and inner-city youth. Because this behavior typically does not emerge until adolescence, the short-term goals for elementary school children were to reduce aggression, reduce associated risk factors (that is, poor social problem-solving skills), and increase associated protective factors (that is, school achievement). Risk and protective factors were considered secondary outcomes, and children's aggression was considered a primary outcome. Whether the intervention "worked" or not hinged on whether we were able to demonstrate reductions in aggressive behavior relative to the control condition for the most aggressive children in our sample. Our conceptualization of effectiveness hinged on demonstrated behavior change in aggression as a proxy for later violence. However, across a range of prevention studies there is substantial variability in how effectiveness is conceptualized, suggesting a need for greater precision. Of particular importance are differences in specificity of outcomes and the clinical significance of findings.

Specificity of Outcomes Vis-à-vis Aggression and Violence

There is remarkably little consistency across aggression and violence prevention studies in specificity of outcomes. In many cases, the distinction between aggression and violence is blurred, although violence is usually considered a more extreme form of aggression. Most frequently, the term "aggression" is used to describe children's behavior and the term "youth violence" is used to describe adolescent behavior (Guerra and Knox, 2002). Following this logic, we would expect programs focused on younger children to include measures of their aggressive behavior and programs focused on adolescents to include measures of more serious violent behavior as evidence that the program works. In practice, even violence prevention programs for adolescents rarely measure actual effects on reducing violent behavior per se, in part due to the low base rates of serious violence, although many programs assess some type of aggressive behavior. Program evaluations also frequently include a range of other measures of associated risk factors, including individual attributes (self control), related behaviors (delinquent acts), and sanctions (school suspensions).

Clinical Significance of Findings

Along with the specific constructs and measures relied upon to assess the outcomes of youth violence prevention programming, of great importance in determining whether a program "works" is the particular criterion used to make that judgment. The common practice of reporting only statistical significance has clear limitations. Indeed, it is important to consider both statistical and clinical significance. For example, is the treated group now indistinguishable from a normative population, whereas the non-treated group is not (Kendall, Marrs-Garcia, Nath, and Sheldrick, 1999)? Has the quality of life of the treated group improved in ways that the quality of life of the non-treated group has not (Gladis, Gosch, Dishuk, and Crits-Christoph, 1999)?

In the MACS, the primary measure used to assess changes in aggression was a linear composite of ratings made by both teachers and peers. The teacher report measure was Achenbach's (1991) Teacher Report Form (TRF) of the Child Behavior Checklist. As a clinical rating scale, the TRF produces T score equivalents of raw scores that indicate whether a target child's problem behaviors are present to a degree similar to typical children referred for clinical psychological treatment. One critical finding in the evaluation of the MACS was that in the moderate resource schools, the full level C intervention for the younger age group produced general tendencies toward less aggression compared to control, whereas in the low-resource schools, the reverse was observed. These divergent results were produced through analyses of the composite (teacher report plus peer rating) aggression measure. However, when considered with respect to clinical status levels using just the TRF, a different pattern emerged. Here, in both the moderate- and low-resource schools, the full intervention actually produced beneficial effects on clinical status levels for the younger age group. In the moderate-resource schools, 18.3 percent of children in the full intervention moved from clinical status to sub-clinical status compared to 3.1 percent of the controls. In the low-resource schools, the proportions were 10.3 percent and 3.4 percent, respectively. This result, which demonstrates effects of the intervention on very high-risk youth, was masked by analyses examining more general trends in the different samples.

NEW DIRECTIONS FOR EVALUATION • DOI: 10.1002/ev

Rethinking the Question: For Whom

As we have discussed previously, it is likely that interventions have different effects for different individuals based on several key factors. Even absent specific hypotheses for differential effects, it is important to begin to enumerate potential individual level moderators of intervention effectiveness, the "for whom" in understanding outcomes of aggression and violence prevention programs. We propose three important potential individual moderators that have been examined to some degree in violence prevention research. These are developmental timing, predisposition to aggression, and peer social status.

Developmental Timing. From a developmental perspective, comprehensive youth development and violence prevention programming should begin before birth and continue into adolescence and young adulthood (Weissberg and Greenberg, 1998). From a policy and practice perspective, it is often necessary to select specific ages for priority funding in order to focus resources on age groups most likely to benefit from the intervention. This suggests the importance of identifying whether certain interventions are more effective during certain developmental periods. Depending on the type of intervention, it is possible to make specific hypotheses in relation to developmental timing. For example, we would expect interventions aimed at changing peer group norms to be more effective during adolescence when the influence of the peer group is most salient.

In some cases, a general type of intervention such as social-problem solving or social-skills training has been used across multiple age groups. There has been consensus that aggression prevention interventions should start early, in part due to the relative stability of children's aggression from the early school years (Huesmann, Eron, Lefkowitz, and Walder, 1984). This "earlier is better" standard has also been supported by studies suggesting that children who begin their aggression early are more likely to continue this behavior into adolescence and are more likely to develop entrenched negative behaviors that are difficult to change as they get older (Dishion and Patterson, 1992; Moffitt, 1993). This would suggest that early intervention is recommended, but particularly for those children already displaying aggressive behavioral tendencies (that is, secondary or selective prevention). In fact, the early starter-late starter model (Moffitt, 1993) also identifies a late starter group that begins antisocial behavior in adolescence, suggesting that, for these youth, intervening during the adolescent years is recommended.

Most studies that have considered the moderating influence of age have examined effects within a specific age period, typically based on school level (elementary, middle, high school). In the MACS study, we examined whether outcomes varied for children who began the program in the early (Grades 2–3) versus late (Grades 5–6) elementary school years. We found that the comprehensive program that included children, teachers, peers, and families was effective but only for the younger age group, supporting the emphasis on early intervention. However, we did not include a middle school or high school sample in the intervention study.

In a recent meta-analysis of the effects of social skills training (SST) for students with externalizing behavior disorders, Gresham and others (forthcoming) reported a U-shaped curvilinear relation between the efficacy of SST and positive student behavior change as a function of age. Specifically, age moderated the effectiveness of SSTs, whereby SSTs were most effective during the early childhood and the adolescent years and less effective during the middle childhood years. As the authors discuss, it may be that SSTs during the early childhood years are affecting the "early starters" and SSTs during the adolescent years are affecting the "late starters," while SSTs during middle school years are actually affecting the early starters whose aggression has become more chronic over time and hence more resistant.

Predisposition to Aggression. An important consideration for prevention programming is the extent to which change occurs among the more aggressive youth. Indeed, many large-scale evaluation studies have reported significant effects for all youth (as part of primary or universal preventive efforts) as well as for subgroups of more aggressive youth participating in more intensive secondary or selective prevention programming (Conduct Problems Prevention Research Group, 2002). In the MACS study, significant reductions in aggression were only found for the high-risk more aggressive children who participated in the most intensive intervention programming, although both low- and high-risk children participated in the universal classroom enhancement program offered at all levels of intervention.

In addition to examining whether program outcomes vary as a function of an individual's baseline level of aggression, it is also likely that outcomes may vary within the more aggressive group. In other words, there may be specific subgroups of aggressive children who respond differentially to a particular intervention. For example, one subgroup may be related to whether or not other problem behaviors or disorders are present (that is, comorbidity). On the one hand, we might expect that aggressive children with comorbid problems or disorders would be particularly resistant to intervention efforts, given the complexity and extent of their problems. However, intervention effectiveness may also depend on the nature of the comorbid disorders. For example, some studies have found that children with comorbid conduct problems and depression were actually more responsive to interventions than children with conduct problems alone (Beauchaine, Gartner, and Hagen, 2000). It may be that comorbidity is more problematic when aggression or conduct problems are linked with problems that might increase the explosive or chronic nature of aggression and violence (Lynam, 1998).

Peer Social Status. One of the most robust findings in the literature is the link between peer rejection and aggression: rejection and aggression are highly correlated and rejection exacerbates aggression among children initially disposed to behave aggressively (Dodge and Pettit, 2003; Newcomb, Bukowski, and Pattee, 1993). The negative consequences of aggression within a child's peer group presumably should provide a source of motivation for children to decrease their aggression. However, over the past decade, several studies have identified a subgroup of aggressive children who are able to maintain a popular status among their peers (for example, Farmer and others, 2003; Rodkin, Farmer, Pearl, and Van Acker, 2000).

Analyses of data from the MACS illustrate this possibility. Boxer, Huesmann, Hanish, and Guerra (forthcoming) examined pre-test and post-test peer-rated indicators of aggression and popularity in the late intervention. Across conditions, the correlation between aggression and popularity became more positive from pre-test to post-test, consistent with earlier studies. Interestingly, however, the amount of change in the correlation was statistically significant only in the intervention conditions and not in the control condition. Follow-up analyses suggested that youth who began the MACS late intervention program at relatively high levels of popularity (greater than 0.5 SD above the mean) were more likely to increase in their aggressiveness in active treatment than in the control condition. In contrast, low-popularity youth showed decreases in their aggression in the context of intervention.

Rethinking the Question: Under What Conditions

Implementing violence prevention programs in real-world settings also requires attention to contextual conditions that may facilitate or interfere with prevention outcomes. Although studies examining the moderating role of contextual factors are limited, previous research suggests the importance of two broad categories of contextual moderators. These are conditions that support the learning and maintenance of aggression and conditions that interfere with high-quality implementation of the intervention. Because many aggression and violence prevention programs (including the MACS program) are implemented in school settings, we use school context to illustrate how these moderators may affect outcomes.

Conditions That Support the Learning and Maintenance of Aggression. Some school-based preventive interventions focus on individual skill building or promoting competencies through classroom-level curricula. Other school-based programs emphasize changing contextual conditions that support aggression, such as teacher reinforcement for aggression and school-wide norms supporting aggression. More recently, the emphasis on comprehensive programming has led to programs that seek to change both individual and contextual factors, as illustrated in the MACS study. However, regardless of the extent to which contextual conditions are addressed, it is unlikely that all conditions that support the learning and maintenance of aggression can be considered in any single program—in many cases, these conditions are simply beyond the scope of school-based prevention (that is, poverty, neighborhood violence). Still, it is important to enumerate those conditions that are most likely to affect whether a program works or does not work.

The learning and maintenance of aggression is more likely under conditions where aggression is seen as "normative" (that is, the extent to which it is seen as acceptable in a given setting) and where there are ample opportunities for reinforcement. This was supported in the MACS study. As Henry and others (2000) report, children's aggressive behavior was more likely to improve when they were in classrooms with lower levels of normative beliefs supporting aggression, and their aggressive behavior was more likely to escalate when they were in classrooms with higher levels of normative support. This finding is also consistent with a recent study by Aber and others (2002). In their evaluation of the Resolving Conflict Creatively program, a classroom-based elementary school program, they found positive effects on aggression only in classrooms where children's normative beliefs supporting aggression were low.

We also would expect school-based interventions to be less effective in classrooms where teachers reinforce children's aggression (for example, through increased attention) and in schools with inconsistent sanctions for aggression and higher levels of tolerance for such behavior (if these conditions are not addressed directly by the intervention). Studies have shown that classroom and school climates that reinforce aggression serve to foster and sustain more severe forms of aggression (Greene, 2005; Kallestad and Olweus, 2003). Supports and sanctions for aggression may also contribute to an overall school climate that fosters or inhibits the development of aggression (McEvoy and Welker, 2002).

Conditions That Interfere with High-Quality Implementation of the Intervention. Perhaps the most important finding in the MACS intervention, to date, is that intervention outcomes were moderated by level of school adversity. Positive effects were found only in schools with at least moderate levels of resources, and negative effects were found under some conditions but only in schools with low levels of resources (although positive effects for clinical significance were noted across both moderate and low-resource schools). The finding that school adversity moderated outcomes is consistent with a number of aggression and violence prevention efforts that have demonstrated poorer outcomes in more distressed and disadvantaged settings (Aber and others, 2002; Hughes and others, 2005). Ironically, although interventions may be most needed in low-resource schools, the realities of these low-resource schools may also make these interventions less effective.

It is possible that these interventions are less effective because of the multiplicity of risk factors that exist in more disadvantaged settings: even the most comprehensive interventions are unlikely to address this array of factors. However, it is also important to consider the ways in which adversity may interfere with high quality implementation of interventions. For instance, teachers and administrators in low-resource schools are likely to struggle to "survive" rather than thrive. Children may come to school ill-prepared for the day, teachers may feel overburdened with challenges of teaching in a low-resource environment, and schools are likely to be under-staffed and have relatively high rates of turnover. The addition of a new vio-lence prevention curriculum or program may tax an already overburdened system (Gresham, 1989; Telzrow, McNamara, and Hollinger, 2000).

Conclusions and Future Directions

In spite of numerous evaluations of youth violence prevention programs and the urgent need for evidence-based practices, there are still relatively few documented "best practices" to guide policies and programs. Even consid-ering interventions with evidence of effectiveness in more than one setting, it is still unlikely that such programs work equally well for all youth under all conditions. Indeed, most "best practice" guidelines suggested by agen-cies such as the CDC (Thornton and others, 2000) as well as various researchers (for example, Boxer and Dubow, 2002; Tolan and Guerra, 1994) typically are main effects recommendations. They do not take into account the critical issues of "what works and what does not, for whom, and under what conditions."

To provide greater clarity and direction for practice in youth violence prevention, we suggest that program evaluations focus attention not only on outcomes, but also on moderators of outcomes. As we have illustrated with findings from the Metropolitan Area Child Study, evaluations that do not consider specific moderators may deem a program to be ineffective when, in fact, it was effective, but only for some children. In the MACS example, the full intervention was effective only for younger more aggres-sive children in schools with greater resources. However, when clinical sig-nificance was considered, the program was effective in reducing the aggression levels of the most extremely aggressive youth to normative lev-els regardless of school resources. It may be that school resources are par-ticularly important for implementation overall, but within schools a teacher with one or two highly aggressive children might also be motivated to implement an intervention beyond limitations of school resources.

Because there are numerous violence prevention programs that have shown efficacy with distinct populations, such as young children at risk for serious conduct problems (Webster-Stratton and Reid, 2003) or older ado-lescents already engaged in delinquent behavior (Henggeler and others, 1996), we propose that researchers focus on second-level evaluation studies to assess the effectiveness of those interventions across different settings and for different intervention groups. For example, does multi-systemic therapy work equally well for adolescents living in the inner-city as well as in rural settings? Does it matter whether services are provided by front-line direct care workers, by seasoned or less experienced teachers, or by clinical psy-chologists? Certainly these types of questions are being addressed by the groups who have developed efficacious interventions. The thrust of our recommendation is that it might be most useful for others interested in ascertaining program effects to focus on the portability of existing strong programs and to identify target groups for whom existing interventions are not effective prior to developing new programs focused on groups not well served by current interventions. Not only is this an important next step for youth violence prevention programs, but it should add to literature on program effectiveness across multiple interventions that target a range of problems.

References

Aber, J. L., Jones, S. B., Brown, J. L., Chaudry, N., and Samples, F. "Resolving Conflict Creatively: Evaluating the Developmental Effects of a School-Based Violence Prevention Program in Neighborhood and Classroom Context." *Development and Psychopathology,* 2002, *10,* 187–213.

Achenbach, T. M. *Teacher Report Form.* Burlington, Vt.: Achenbach System of Empirically Based Assessment, 1991.

Beauchaine, T. P., Gartner, J., and Hagen, B. "Comorbid Depression and Heart Rate Variability as Predictors of Aggressive and Hyperactive Symptom Responsiveness During Inpatient Treatment of Conduct-Disordered, ADHD Boys." *Aggressive Behavior,* 2000, *26,* 425–441.

Boxer, P., and Dubow, E. F. "A Social-Cognitive Information-Processing Model for School-Based Aggression Reduction and Prevention Programs: Issues for Research and Practice." *Applied and Preventive Psychology,* 2002, *10,* 177–192.

Boxer, P., Guerra, N. G., Huesmann, L. R., and Morales, J. "Proximal Peer-Level Effects of a Small-Group Selected Prevention Program on Aggression in Elementary School Children: An Investigation of the Peer Contagion Hypothesis." *Journal of Abnormal Child Psychology,* 2005, *33,* 325–338.

Boxer, P., Huesmann, L. R., Hanish, L. D., and Guerra, N. G. "Sociometric Popularity in School-Based Aggression Prevention: Getting Cool by Getting Tough." *Journal of Child Clinical Psychology,* forthcoming.

Chan, L. S., Kipke, M. D., Schneir, A., and others. *Preventing Violence and Related Health-Risking Social Behaviors in Adolescents: Summary.* Evidence Report/Technology Assessment No. 107. AHRQ Publication Number 04-E032-1. Rockville, Md.: Agency for Health Care Research and Quality, Sept. 2004.

Cicchetti, D., and Rogosch, F. A. "Equifinality and Mutifinality in Developmental Psychopathology." *Development and Psychopathology,* 1996, *8,* 597–600.

Conduct Problems Prevention Research Group. "Evaluation of the First Three Years of the Fast Track Prevention Trial with Children at High Risk for Adolescent Conduct Problems." *Journal of Abnormal Child Psychology,* 2002, *30,* 19–35.

Dodge, K. A., and Pettit, G. S. "A Biopsychosocial Model of the Development of Chronic Conduct Problems in Adolescence." *Developmental Psychology,* 2003, *39,* 349–371.

Dishion, T. J., McCord, J., and Poulin, F. "When Interventions Harm: Peer Groups and Problem Behavior." *American Psychologist,* 1999, *54,* 755–764.

Dishion, T. J., and Patterson, G. R. "Age Effects in Parent Training Outcome." *Behavior Therapy,* 1992, *23,* 719–729.

Dodge, K. A., and Pettit, G. S. "A Biopsychosocial Model of the Development of Chronic Conduct Problems in Adolescence." *Developmental Psychology,* 2003, *39,* 349–371.

Fagan, A. A., and Mihalic, S. "Strategies for Enhancing the Adoption of School-Based Prevention Programs: Lessons Learned from the Blueprints for Violence Prevention Replications of the Life Skills Training Program." *Journal of Community Psychology,* 2003, *31,* 235–253.

Farmer, T. W., Estell, D. B., Bishop, J. L., O'Neal, K. K., and Cairns, B. D. "Rejected Bullies or Popular Leaders? The Social Relations of Aggressive Subtypes of Rural African American Early Adolescents." *Developmental Psychology,* 2003, *39,* 992–1004.

Farrell, A. D., Meyer, A. L., and White, K. S. "Evaluation of Responding in Positive and Peaceful Ways (RIPP): A School-Based Prevention Program for Reducing Violence Among Urban Adolescents." *Journal of Clinical Child Psychology,* 2001, *30,* 451–463.

Frick, P. J. "Effective Interventions for Children and Adolescents with Conduct Disorder." *Canadian Journal of Psychiatry,* 2001, *46,* 597–608.

Gladis, M. M., Gosch, E. A., Dishuk, N. M., and Crits-Christoph, P. "Quality of Life: Expanding the Scope of Clinical Significance." *Journal of Consulting and Clinical Psychology,* 1999, *67,* 320–331.

Greene, M. B. "Reducing Violence and Aggression in Schools." *Trauma, Violence, & Abuse,* 2005, *6,* 236–253.

Gresham, F. M. "Assessment of Treatment Integrity in School Consultation and Peripheral Intervention." *School Psychology Review,* 1989, *18,* 37–50.

Gresham, F. M., Barreras, R. B., Cook, C. R., Crews, S. D., and Kern, L. "Social Skills Training with Secondary EBD Students: Current Status and Future Directions." *Journal of Emotional and Behavioral Disorders,* forthcoming.

Guerra, N. G., Boxer, P., and Kim, T. E. "A Cognitive-ecological Approach to Serving Students with Emotional and Behavioral Disorders: Application to Aggressive Behavior." *Journal of Emotional and Behavioral Disorders,* forthcoming.

Guerra, N. G., and Huesmann, L. R. "A Cognitive-Ecological Model of Aggression." *Revue Internationale de Psychologie Sociale,* 2004, *17,* 177–203.

Guerra, N. G., and Knox, L. "Violence." *Encyclopedia of Crime and Justice.* New York: MacMillan, 2002, 1649–1655.

Henggeler, S. W., Cunningham, B., Pickrel, S. G., Schoenwald, S. K., and Brondino, M. J. "Multisystemic Therapy: An Effective Violence Prevention Approach for Serious Offenders." *Journal of Adolescence,* 1996, *19,* 47–61.

Henry, D., Guerra, N. G., Huesmann, L. R., Tolan, P. H., VanAcker, R., and Eron, L. D. "Normative Influences on Aggression in Urban Elementary School Classrooms." *American Journal of Community Psychology,* 2000, *28,* 59–81.

Huesmann, L. R., Eron, L. D., Lefkowitz, M. M., and Walder, L. O. "Stability of Aggression over Time and Generations." *Developmental Psychology,* 1984, *20,* 1120–1134.

Hughes, J. N., Cavell, T. A., Meehan, B. T., Zhang, D., and Collie, C. "Adverse School Context Moderates the Outcomes of Selective Interventions for Aggressive Children." *Journal of Consulting and Clinical Psychology,* 2005, *73,* 731–736.

Kallestad, J. H., and Olweus, D. "Predicting Teachers' and Schools' Implementation of the Olweus Bullying Prevention Program: A Multilevel Study." *Prevention & Treatment,* 2003, *6*(1), Article 21. http://content.apa.org/journals/pre/6/1/21a.html.

Kazdin, A. E. "The State of Child and Adolescent Psychotherapy Research." *Child and Adolescent Mental Health,* 2002, *7,* 53–59.

Kendall, P. C., Marrs-Garcia, A., Nath, S. R., and Sheldrick, R. C. "Normative Comparisons for the Evaluation of Clinical Significance." *Journal of Consulting and Clinical Psychology,* 1999, *67,* 285–299.

Lynam, D. R. "Early Identification of the Fledgling Psychopath: Locating the Psychopathic Child in the Current Nomenclature." *Journal of Abnormal Psychology,* 1998, *107*(4), 566–575.

McEvoy, A., and Welker, R. "Antisocial Behavior, Academic Failure, and School Climate: A Critical Review." *Journal of Emotional and Behavioral Disorders,* 2002, *8,* 130–140.

Metropolitan Area Child Study Research Group. "A Cognitive-ecological Approach to Preventing Aggression in Urban Settings: Initial Outcomes for High-Risk Children." *Journal of Consulting and Clinical Psychology,* 2002, *70,* 179–194.

Mihalic, S., Fagan, A. A., Irwin, K., Ballard, D., and Elliott, D. *Blueprints for Violence Prevention*. Washington, D.C.: Office of Juvenile Justice and Delinquency Prevention, 2004.

Moffitt, T. E. "Adolescence-Limited and Life-Course-Persistent Antisocial Behavior: A Developmental Taxonomy." *Psychological Review*, 1993, *100*, 674–701.

Newcomb, A. F., Bukowski, W. M., Pattee, L. "Children's Peer Relations: A Meta-Analytic Review of Popular, Rejected, Neglected, Controversial, and Average Sociometric Status." *Psychological Bulletin*, 1993, *113*, 99–128.

Rodkin, P. C., Farmer, T. W., Pearl, R., and Van Acker, R. "Heterogeneity of Popular Boys: Antisocial and Prosocial Configurations." *Developmental Psychology*, 2000, *36*, 14–24.

Telzrow, C. F., McNamara, K., and Hollinger, C. L. "Fidelity of Problem-Solving Implementation and Relationship to Student Performance." *School Psychology Review*, 2000, *29*, 443–461.

Thornton, T. N., Craft, C. A., Dahlberg, L. L., Lynch, B. S., and Baer, K. *Best Practices of Youth Violence Prevention: A Sourcebook for Community Action*. Atlanta, Ga.: Centers for Disease Control and Prevention, 2000.

Tolan, P., and Guerra, N. G. *What Works in Reducing Youth Violence*. Boulder, Colo.: Center for Study and Prevention of Violence, 1994.

Webster-Stratton, C., and Reid, M. J. "The Incredible Years Parents, Teachers, and Children Training Series: A Multifaceted Treatment Approach for Young Children with Conduct Problems." In A. E. Kazdin and J. R. Weisz (eds.), *Evidence-Based Psychotherapies for Children and Adolescents*. New York: Guilford, 2003, 224–240.

Weissberg, R. P., and Greenberg, M. T. "School and Community Competence-Enhancement and Prevention Programs." In W. Damon (Series ed.), I. E. Siegel, and K. A. Renninger (Vol. eds.), *Handbook of Child Psychology: Vol. 4. Child Psychology in Practice* (5th ed.), New York: Wiley, 1998, 877–954.

Wilson, S. J., Lipsey, M. W., and Derzon, J. H. "The Effects of School-Based Intervention Programs on Aggressive Behavior: A Meta-Analysis." *Journal of Consulting and Clinical Psychology*, 2003, *71*, 136–149.

NANCY G. GUERRA *is professor of psychology at the University of California Riverside and Principal Investigator of the Academic Center of Excellence on Youth Violence Prevention funded by the Centers for Disease Control and Prevention.*

PAUL BOXER *is assistant professor of psychology at the University of New Orleans and adjunct faculty associate in the Research Center for Group Dynamics at the University of Michigan.*

CLAYTON R. COOK *is a doctoral student in the school psychology program at the University of California Riverside.*

*This chapter discusses a multisite program evaluation
in elementary schools that incorporated playground
observations to document student behavior. A number of
challenges are discussed, some of which were consistent
with observer reactivity effects long documented in the
literature, while others we believe were unique to this
particular setting and provide a cautionary tale for
those collecting school-based observation data.*

Who Is Watching the Watchers?
The Challenge of Observing Peer
Interactions on Elementary School
Playgrounds

Cynthia Hudley

Direct observation in natural settings has been recognized for nearly a century (Thomas, 1929) as an important methodology to capture the nuances of children's behavior for research, clinical assessment, and program evaluation. These ecologically valid descriptive data complement more widely used behavior rating scales to evaluate the impact of intervention programming on children's aggressive behavior. While observation data make an undeniable contribution to evaluation findings, particularly for programs of behavior change, the validity and reliability of observation data have been debated for more than half a century (Arrington, 1943; Johnson and Bolstad, 1973). This paper discusses challenges encountered in a multisite, multimethod evaluation of an intervention program to reduce aggressive behavior in elementary schools. The evaluation design incorporated multiple sources of data, including playground observations. The observation data were difficult to collect and challenging to integrate into the full complement of evaluation findings. After briefly reviewing the literature on the costs and benefits of observation data that guided the decision to include an observation component in the evaluation design, the chapter will describe the evaluation project, a series of apparently unique, previously unreported difficulties in implementing the observation component, and the lessons learned from those difficulties.

New Directions for Evaluation, no. 110, Summer 2006   © Wiley Periodicals, Inc.
Published online in Wiley InterScience (www.interscience.wiley.com) • DOI: 10.1002/ev.188

Why Observation?

Direct observation has become one of the preeminent techniques for assessing behavior problems in children because it is the best, if not the only, way to capture peer interactions in the natural environment. Observation data can yield valuable information about the functional significance of a child's aggression and thus help understand how best to intervene. For example, if a child is using aggression to purposefully dominate peers, training in assertive communication will likely have little effect or will serve to worsen the behavior. However, if a third grader is highly reactively aggressive because he lacks the social communication skills to successfully enter a play setting, training in positive and assertive social skills may improve his peer interactions. Similarly, only observations can yield real-time information about children's use of social skills and strategies in the context of peer interactions. This last point is especially important in evaluation design because programs of behavior change typically focus on teaching children more effective strategies and skills. Instruction and experiences in the intervention setting should translate into changes in behavior when the child interacts with the peer group using the newly trained skills. Direct observations that capture these peer interactions are central to understanding not only changes in behavior but also the role of the intervention in effecting those behavior changes.

However, direct observation data can be most useful when incorporated into an evaluation design that includes multiple informants and multiple methods (McMahon and Frick, 2005). The effectiveness of a behavior change intervention will ultimately be judged by a variety of people whose perspectives can be measured with behavior rating scales, interviews, peer sociometric questionnaires, and self-report instruments. Teacher perspectives are of particular interest, given that teacher judgments are a frequent metric for defining problem behaviors, and all children in elementary schools are subject to teacher judgments. Intervention programs for elementary school children's aggression—whether school based, home based, or community based—that do not result in changes in teachers' perceptions cannot be considered completely effective in eliminating some of the negative consequences of aggressive behavior (school disciplinary action, time lost in class, negative stereotypes). Similarly, Hudley and others (2001) agree that assessments of childhood aggression should include peer perceptions. Peer perceptions are at least as effective at predicting problems in later life as are teacher reports and are more effective than parent reports. Self-reports are also necessary when evaluating cognitive-behavioral interventions to reduce childhood aggression. These programs address children's thinking (attributions, normative beliefs) and emotions (anger control) and presume that changes in behavior result from changes in cognitive and affective processes that lead to changes in the use of social strategies; self report measures are indispensable for assessing changes in these underlying psychological processes that might account for any observed changes in strategy use and behavior.

Perhaps the strongest argument for multiple evaluation methods concerns outcomes. Studies examining the predictive power of various measures and informants show clearly that different methods (observations, parent and teacher ratings, measures of parenting processes) can differentially predict long-term life outcomes (Patterson and Forgatch, 1995). Thus, designs that incorporate multiple measures and multiple informants are likely to be the most authoritative in evaluating behavior change, the processes responsible for that change, and the long-term prospects for positive adjustment by the program participants.

This brief review is intended to demonstrate the positive value of observations for evaluating aggression reduction programs in elementary schools, as well as the importance of using multiple data sources and methods in evaluation designs. However, there is another side of this discussion. Although effects do not always appear, under some conditions the experience of being observed significantly influences the behavior being observed (Haynes and Horn, 1982), making observation data potentially inconsistent with data from other sources. A long history of research has documented the problems of participant reactivity or changes in behavior in response to an awareness of monitoring. Most important for evaluating aggression or other inappropriate behavior, the typical effect of reactivity is a move toward social desirability, which can be expected to substantially reduce the display of the behavior of interest. Some early work with aggressive elementary school children suggested that the presence of an adult observer caused children to change their behavior in the classroom as well as in play settings (Hay, Nelson, and Hay, 1977; Martin, Gelfand, and Hartmann, 1971).

On playgrounds, older elementary children are more aware of observers and more likely to change their behavior as well as remove themselves to places where they cannot be observed (Lagerspetz, Bjorkqvist, and Peltonen, 1988; Sluckin, 1981). Reactivity to observers also seems to differ according to whether the observer is familiar or a stranger, but the evidence is equivocal as to which is the better choice. On the one hand, an observer who is familiar to participants may be less salient on the playground and therefore less obtrusive (Merrell, 2003). On the other hand, an observer with a history of contact with students may influence behavior on the basis of that history. For example, in early laboratory studies a prior history of negative interactions between an observer and target child predicted more problem behaviors when the observer was present, and a history of positive interactions caused a positive change in behavior during observation (Marsh and Hedley, 1975).

In more recent years, the problem of observer intrusiveness on the playground has been addressed with the introduction of remote video recording and wireless microphones worn by a target child (Pepler and Craig, 1995). A camera overlooking the playground but not visible to the students receives the audio signal for simultaneous audio and video recording. Such a strategy may eliminate the presence of an additional adult on the playground, but represents another type of intrusion that can carry unique kinds of reactivity. The balance of this chapter presents the evaluation of an aggression reduction program as an example of the mixed blessings of observation data as one part of a multimethod evaluation and lessons learned from the experience.

A Multisite Evaluation of the BrainPower Program

The project described here was a multisite, multimethod evaluation of the BrainPower Program (Hudley, 1994; Hudley and others, 1998; Hudley and Friday, 1996; Hudley and Graham, 1993). The program is a twelve lesson cognitive-behavioral intervention curriculum for middle and upper elementary grade students (grades 3–6) that is delivered through small group instruction. The program goal is to reduce peer directed, reactive aggression by changing children's attributions of hostile intent in peer interactions and providing them with more effective social strategies. Groups of six students met twice weekly with a team of two group leaders in sixty-minute sessions separate from the regular classroom for a total of twelve sessions. Each group consisted of four highly aggressive and two average, nonaggressive students. Nonaggressive students were included to avoid stigmatization and to guard against deviancy training or iatrogenic effects for the aggressive children. Nonaggressive students also served as positive peer models while they themselves had the opportunity to reappraise their attitudes about the aggressive students as they progressed through the program.

A prior project, an efficacy trial conducted in a clinical setting, demonstrated that changing children's attributions indeed changed their aggressive behavior (Hudley and Graham, 1993). The multisite evaluation project discussed here, an effectiveness trial, was designed to determine how useful the program might be for school sites (Hudley, 2003; Hudley and others, 1998). Four elementary schools in southern California, selected to obtain a reasonable representation of the ethnic makeup of public schools in the area at the time, served as evaluation sites. The participating schools enrolled virtually 100 percent ethnic minority students whose economic circumstances ranged from lower middle class to public welfare recipients. However, the intervention program served only students who were English proficient, and as a result African American student participants were the predominant majority in the intervention and evaluation projects.

Evaluation Design and Measures. Intervention participants, selected through a combination of teacher ratings and peer sociometric nominations, totaled 256 aggressive (64 per school) and 128 nonaggressive (32 per school) third to sixth grade minority males. Students, aggressive and nonaggressive, were randomly assigned to one of three groups: the experimental

NEW DIRECTIONS FOR EVALUATION • DOI: 10.1002/ev

intervention (24 aggressive, 12 nonaggressive per school), a placebo condition that trained students in nonsocial problem solving and critical thinking skills (24 aggressive, 12 nonaggressive per school), or a pre- and post-test only comparison group (16 aggressive and 8 nonaggressive per school). Baseline data were collected prior to the start of intervention group meetings, and data were collected again within six weeks of the end of each student's participation in a small group (and at that same time for the no-treatment group) and semiannually for the following eighteen months.

The evaluation incorporated multiple sources of data. Students' self reports were measured with written hypothetical scenarios of peer interactions that result in a negative outcome for the subject. Situations include destruction of property (a ruined homework paper), physical harm (a hard push by a peer), and social rejection (a planned meeting with a peer who never showed up). Students were asked to rate the level of peers' intentionality, their own feelings of anger, and to specify their most likely response from a list of six behaviors that ranged from completely benign to physical aggression. Teachers rated aggressive behavior using the teacher form of the Social Skills Rating System (Gresham and Elliott, 1990), an instrument that yields subscale scores for perceptions of self-control ("controls temper in conflict situations with peers"), cooperation ("ignores peer distractions when doing class work"), and externalizing behavior ("fights with others"). Although teachers were aware that some students participated in small group activities, all teachers were blind to students' group assignments. To measure school disciplinary actions, administrative logs were reviewed for the school year immediately preceding the intervention program and annually for the two years following the intervention.

Trained observers conducted playground observations during a twelve-week period at pre-test, post-test, and one year follow up. Each student was observed for five minutes during each of four separate observation sessions (a total of twenty minutes per child) during recess, lunch, or physical education activities. For each child, observations had to take place in at least two distinct settings. Observers used time sampling to code behavior at thirty-second intervals to maximize the opportunity to observe aggression. Thus, for every child we planned for forty observation data points that recorded the target child's behavior (one of twelve categories of aggressive, prosocial, or neutral behavior), peers' behavior (if present), and context of the behaviors (peer interactive, peer independent, non-peer interactive, solitary). Data were recorded on a coding sheet attached to a clip board. Each observer wore headphones connected to a small tape player that could not be seen (for example, hidden in a pocket) to provide a thirty-second cue.

Challenges for Implementation at the Schools

The evaluation project was presented to the four participating schools as a part of the full package of the intervention curriculum. I first presented the curriculum and the need for evaluation research to the four principals and subsequently to the faculties at each of the schools. Overall, the project was enthusiastically welcomed; teachers were convinced that they had more students who might qualify than available spaces in the intervention groups. As well, each school agreed to the three group evaluation design that included students who would not receive the aggression reduction curriculum and site staff unaware of student status as either intervention or placebo group (because they provided rating data, teachers remained blind to students' status in the evaluation).

Two challenges arose initially, both of which shaped the collection of observation data. All schools agreed that some form of observation data would be valuable in conjunction with teacher ratings and school records. However, no schools agreed to have students audiotaped using wireless technology, and two schools were extremely reluctant to allow outside observers onto the playground. At the time of this evaluation (well before the introduction of MP3 players and iPod devices), wireless electronics were not as pervasive and familiar as they are today, and, in general, electronic devices of any kind (beepers, video games, Walkman radios) were considered contraband at elementary schools. Schools also raised concerns about student and parent confidentiality issues if children's conversations were taped. Therefore, schools were unwilling to compromise on the issue of wireless recording. The evaluation team suggested placing observers on the playground, and two schools wanted teachers to serve as the observers. These two schools, both located in high crime neighborhoods in the Los Angeles area, were extremely concerned that their schools remain completely closed campuses. I was interested in retaining schools serving students from communities that were challenged by crime. However, I was concerned about student reactivity to familiar teachers (as described above) as well as the potential for teachers' biased perceptions based on children's prior behavior (Hudley and others, 2001). I much preferred less familiar, if not completely unfamiliar, observers. As well, members of the evaluation team, none of whom were part of the school staff, would have to participate in order to complete observer training and reliability checks. A process of collaborative problem solving led us to a conclusion that was acceptable to all parties. Observations were conducted by adjunct personnel at each site (the after school program leader at two sites, the parent center coordinator, the morning kindergarten teacher aide) with training and reliability duties completed by the research team staff.

Another challenge that arose concerned the timing of the observations. With nearly one hundred participants per school, the initial goal of collecting twenty minutes per child required playground observers to begin as soon as they were trained (November) and continue virtually across the entire school year to complete pre- and post-test observations. This planned schedule accommodated a hiatus in December for holiday activities and school break and another pause in February before the first cohort of students completed intervention activities. However, almost as soon as pretest data collection began, the Los Angeles area experienced a significant (magnitude 6.7) earthquake that closed our participating schools for durations ranging as briefly as two days (two sites) to three weeks (one site).

Lessons Learned for Implementing Observations. These experiences provide three concrete lessons for school-based evaluations. The rise of evaluation paradigms such as empowerment evaluation, responsive evaluation, and democratic evaluation has put the importance of collaborative inquiry front and center in the thinking of program evaluators. When evaluating programs implemented in schools, one goal of collaboration is to fully understand what kinds of data collection activities the local environment can sustain. For example, during the time when this evaluation was conducted, electronic devices such as beepers were a valid indicator of potential delinquent activities. Therefore schools were highly sensitive to the sanctioning and use of electronic equipment by children. Technological advances have reduced this problem significantly (much smaller microphones, mini cameras, and the decline of beeper use among youth), but the lesson remains the same. Evaluation design must be responsive to the concerns and needs of the culture of the site, and in many schools where violence prevention programs are implemented, concerns for safety and security may eliminate relatively common and familiar techniques. Particularly for observations, access to school campuses may be severely restricted, and the decision to use school staff or independent, unknown observers may be dictated to a large extent again by the security needs of the campus.

Finally, our natural disaster reminded us that no design fully accommodates the unexpected. The lesson here is that designs must be responsive to the possibility of a radically revised intervention context. While an earthquake may not be a normative concern in many parts of the country, natural disasters are not the only source of rapid, unexpected change that may occur at a school site. Supportive administrators are transferred; school calendars and daily schedules are revised; and students, classrooms, or entire grade levels may be reassigned to other classrooms or school sites (another of the set of challenges we encountered, this time during an additional follow up period after the primary evaluation was concluded).

Fortunately, for pre-test observations, we were able to prioritize our resources and efforts quickly. We could not alter the intervention curriculum itself without rendering the entire evaluation project invalid. Thus we had to examine exactly how to revise the pre-test data collection in a manner that would allow us to look for change that could be attributed to the curriculum. Every school and the research team immediately understood that to collect post-test data prior to the end of the academic year in which the intervention was conducted, we would have to sacrifice time from the pre-test observation data collection cycle. Our task was identifying the minimum amount of pre-test data that would still allow valid comparisons of student behavior from pre- to post-test and then determining if we had time to complete the necessary observation activities. To remain on schedule to complete intervention activities and post-test assessments for each child, including a full set of observations before the end of the academic year, we collected a reduced set of pre-test observation data (ten minutes, twenty data points per child).

Challenges for Data Collection on the Playground

Once our research design was established and data collection strategies agreed upon, we began training observers. The training included didactic instruction on the meaning of the codes used to record observation information, behavioral indicators of the codes, and time sampling procedures. The coding scheme was designed primarily to capture behavior in peer interactions (hits, pushes, shares, throws, positive play, and so on), but codes were also available for verbalizations (shouts, argues) that required reasonable proximity. The heart of the observer training was a set of graduated experiences in coding actual behavior. Observers began with videotapes of staged activities, with clearly identifiable exemplars at the earliest point of training. Training then moved on to tapes of the actual playground at the school, and the final stages of training were done live on the playground. Once formal data collection began on the playground, observers were blind to both the child's intervention group status and behavior classification (aggressive or nonaggressive). As well, evaluation staff continued reliability checks to assess observer reactivity (Smith and Sheaffer, 1984) or the tendency of observers to decline in performance immediately after training. We also included bi-weekly training meetings with observers to correct for possible observer drift or the tendency to move toward more personalized, idiosyncratic definitions of behavioral codes. These procedures, while successfully training observers, did not mitigate two significant problems with the observations.

Students did not become acclimated to the playground observers. We concluded that the dilemma of familiar versus unfamiliar observers carries potential pitfalls no matter what the choice might be. At the schools using a parent center coordinator and a kindergarten aide, observers were relatively unfamiliar to students; these paraprofessionals were not in regular contact with student participants. At these two schools, students assumed that our observers were school staff who were monitoring their behavior to enforce school rules. At the two schools using after school program staff, some but not all students participated in these programs and knew the staff member. However, none of the staff would have routinely been on the playground at that time of day (recess, lunch time). Thus students were aware that adults were present on the playground out of their normal routine. The further presence of evaluation team staff, typically graduate students, for reliability checks was an additional indicator to students that something out of the routine was taking place. In each of the schools, with familiar and unfamiliar observers, students frequently either went directly to an observer to initiate contact ("What are you doing?" "Why are you here today?" "Who are you?" "What are you writing?") or moved immediately away to another location.

Each of the collaborating schools had dedicated playground staff to monitor child behavior during lunch and recess. As well, at least one teacher (sometimes more in the larger two schools) was present on the playground. The schools and the evaluation teams agreed that students would be relatively familiar with adult monitors on the playground, and thus observers would be minimally disruptive. However, our observers turned out to be the most consistent presence on the playground at two of the four schools. Two of our schools experienced extreme rates of turnover in playground aides. At one school seven different staff filled four positions over the course of the initial year, and by the end of that year, in the midst of post-test assessment, none of the playground aides with whom we had started the year were still on staff at the school. At that school our observer was the parent coordinator, an unfamiliar person; students seemed to assume that the observer was the regular playground staff present to enforce school discipline. A second school had a somewhat lower rate of turnover and a familiar observer, with essentially the same result: students quickly assumed that the after school staff person was also working as a playground aide. At those two schools in particular, observation data yielded extremely low levels of aggressive interactions with peers. Students were either significantly changing their behavior or distancing themselves from the observer. As students moved farther away from the observer, coding verbalizations became difficult, although behaviors remained visible from most vantage points on three of the four campuses.

A different form of reactivity surfaced on our third campus. When examining the data to assess reliability, we became aware that student behavior differed between days when reliability observers were present and days when they were not. Overall, our data showed somewhat less aggressive behavior was coded (push, hit, and so forth) when reliability checks were made. Because the data seemed consistent across both observers with reasonably strong reliability statistics (Cohen's kappa .68–.81) (Bakeman and Gottman, 1986), we speculated that the addition of yet another adult, one who is unfamiliar, probably increased students' tendency to moderate their aggression. However, we still could not rule out the possibility of observer bias. We are left with the possibility that the observer, an after school staff member, displayed reactivity to the reliability coders. Perhaps during observation sessions without reliability assessments this observer might have overestimated aggressive behavior among some students with whom he had prior interactions.

On our fourth campus, earthquake damage to buildings required that portable classrooms be installed on the playground in the middle of pre-test observations, and they remained until post-test observations for the first of two cohorts of participants were completed. This major change in the physical layout of the playground, although unforeseen and uncontrollable, quickly made it clear that the students were able to remove themselves more easily from the presence of observers by using the portable buildings to shield themselves from sight. As should be apparent, observation data were most seriously compromised at this school.

Finally, across the four sites, observers (both primary and reliability observers) raised the concern in training meetings that some students also seemed to vary their behavior according to impression management goals. Some students being observed appeared to stay close to the observer and either tried to start a conversation with the observer or simply refused to play with peers. The observers speculated that these students were concerned about the apparent monitoring and wanted to get a "good report" rather than "get in trouble." Conversely, a small number of students who appeared to be aware that observers were watching the playground if not themselves personally seemed to come to the vicinity of the observer to act out, "show off," or otherwise gain the attention of the observer.

The other significant challenge for observations was the result of irregular access to students due to unexpected, unannounced changes in daily schedules. Recess times were shifted; regular school days were transformed to reduced days, which might eliminate recess, physical education, or lunch time altogether because students went home early. Although a standardized schedule was established at each school at the start of the academic year, changes to this schedule occurred. Opportunities for teacher in-service programs, parent programs, and cultural and holiday celebrations required flexibility in scheduling the school day. Several emergencies, including violent crimes committed in the immediate vicinity of two schools, caused students to be removed from the playground or sent home early. As well, several unanticipated field trips removed children from the playground entirely, often with as little as two days' notice. Finally, some teachers restricted children's activity as a discipline strategy; time out on a bench during lunch or physical education and staying in from recess were common strategies that often restricted our children from the playground. Unfortunately, aggressive students were more often restricted. Sometimes a student was not available on the playground for several days at a time. Perhaps the student was "benched" at lunch one day, went on an unexpected field trip another day, was absent a third, and a fourth day the observation opportunity might have been lost because the school scheduled a reduced day.

Consistently throughout the year, our observers struggled to collect sufficient observations across multiple settings (that is, recess, lunch, physical education) prior to the start of a given student's participation in program activities. As students completed the intervention activities, observers had difficulty completing the target number of observation data points for each child prior to the end of the academic year. We finished the first year with only thirty data points per participant (three sessions of five minutes each), 75 percent of our original goal.

NEW DIRECTIONS FOR EVALUATION • DOI: 10.1002/ev

Lessons Learned from Playground Data Collection. As has been documented over three decades (Sluckin, 1981), students are aware of observation, older children more than younger children. Our unique lesson for this project concerned students' perceptions of observers. Because these students were familiar with adult monitoring, it seems highly possible that they saw our observers as additional playground aides and became more covert in their display of aggression. It is not surprising that students would not want their aggression to be observed, suggesting that perhaps playground observations are no more likely than other methods to capture real-time peer aggression. As well, observations to capture inappropriate behavior among older children (grades 4–6) may yield data that are not valid if students expect discipline sanctions from playground observers. Although the intervention may have reduced impulsive, reactive aggression because children became more strategic and covert in their behavior, in our data the changes described above were consistent across all intervention groups, not specific to those receiving the *BrainPower Program*. Because technology has reduced the need for adults to be physically on the playground to conduct observations, the form of reactivity that we encountered may no longer pose a problem. But we reflect back on the schools' reluctance to have students audiotaped and wonder how those concerns can be addressed so that evaluators might fully deploy the available technology.

Concerning irregular access, as stated earlier, earthquakes or other natural disasters may be non-normative and are unpredictable and uncontrollable; however, evaluation designs that rely on multiple methods and multiple informants are strongest because some data sources may become unexpectedly unavailable. Plans that we made at the initiation of evaluation had to be changed in the face of changing needs and programs in the school. Even with the clarity of hindsight, some possible solutions for schedule disturbances seem to introduce other kinds of disturbances. We might have increased the number of observers on the playground to increase the number of children observed at any one time. However, if the reactivity that we encountered was caused, as we surmise, by the presence of observers, more observers might create even greater distortions of students' behavior. Alternatively, we might have increased the duration of time allocated to conduct observations, but particularly at post-test, we needed to maintain equivalence in the span of time between completing the intervention and conducting the observation. The end of the school year was a deadline that was most decidedly not flexible, and so spacing out observations was not an option.

In the Final Analysis

We persevered in collecting our observation data hoping that the challenges would be overcome and the data would be meaningful. As the prior discussion revealed, the most notable finding was the small proportion of negative behaviors recorded by the observers across the four school sites. According to these data, playground behavior was relatively free of peer conflicts, at least during observation periods. However, the differences between aggressive and nonaggressive students were still substantial, as expected (12 percent versus 3 percent at pre-test assessment). Changes in aggressive behavior from pre- to post-intervention also favored participants in the *BrainPower Program,* as expected; however, these differences were slight (5 percent decrease in observation data points recording aggression for *BrainPower* students compared to 1 percent decrease and 2 percent increase for placebo and control groups, respectively).

We wonder if the data accurately reflected children's experiences on playgrounds because the effects as measured by teacher reports and student self reports indicated that behavior changed significantly and *BrainPower* students significantly reduced their tendency to attribute hostile intent to peers (Hudley, 2003; Hudley and others, 1998). Thus we are left to wonder if the effects of the intervention were not as strong in real time interactions as our alternative sources of data would suggest, or if our measure of real time interactions was sufficiently flawed that we did not adequately capture the changes in behavior. On the other hand, these observation data also leave open the intriguing possibility that simply adding adults to an elementary school playground constitutes a form of intervention for reducing peer directed aggression. Of course, such an intervention would require a rigorous evaluation of its own, with all of the attendant problems of validity that one might imagine if observers were placed on playgrounds to document behavior rather than reduce aggression. At the very least, these data remind us how attractive positive, unexpected adult attention can be for even the most troubled and troubling children. The observational data seem to offer a simple but important lesson for those who wonder if society can really afford smaller classes, smaller schools, and more adults present to meet the needs of children in schools—and if such reforms really are one key to children's healthy development. These data speak in the affirmative. In conclusion, although my certainty in the value of multiple sources of data is in no way shaken by this experience, I share it with others who may appreciate the blessings and the curses of observational data as one source of information on the effectiveness of a school-based intervention program to reduce aggression.

References

Arrington, R. "Time Sampling in Studies of Social Behavior: A Critical Review of Technique and Results with Research Suggestions." *Psychological Bulletin,* 1943, *40,* 81–124.

Bakeman, R., and Gottman, J. *Observing Interaction: An Introduction to Sequential Analysis.* Cambridge, U.K.: Cambridge University Press, 1986.

Gresham F., and Elliott, S. *The Social Skills Rating System.* Circle Pines, Minn.: American Guidance Service, 1990.

Hay, L., Nelson, R., and Hay, W. "The Use of Teachers as Behavioral Observers." *Journal of Applied Behavioral Analysis,* 1977, *10,* 345–348.

Haynes, S., and Horn, W. "Reactivity in Behavioral Observation: A Review." *Behavioral Assessment,* 1982, *4,* 369–385.

Hudley, C. "The Reduction of Childhood Aggression Using the BrainPower Program." In M. Furlong and D. Smith (eds.), *Anger, Hostility and Aggression: Assessment, Prevention, and Intervention Strategies for Youth.* Brandon, Vt.: Clinical Psychology Publishing Co., 1994.

Hudley, C. "Cognitive-Behavioral Intervention with Aggressive Children." In M. Matson (ed), *Neurobiology of Aggression: Understanding and Preventing Violence.* Totowa, N.J.: Humana Press, 2003.

Hudley, C., Britsch, B., Wakefield, W., Smith, T., DeMorat, M., and Cho, S. "An Attribution Retraining Program to Reduce Aggression in Elementary School Students." *Psychology in the Schools,* 1998, *35,* 271–282.

Hudley, C., and Friday, J. "Attributional Bias and Reactive Aggression." *American Journal of Preventive Medicine,* 1996, *12*(Suppl. 1), 75–81.

Hudley, C., and Graham, S. "An Attributional Intervention to Reduce Peer Directed Aggression Among African-American Boys." *Child Development,* 1993, *64,* 124–138.

Hudley, C., Wakefield, W., Britsch, B., Cho, S., Smith, T., and DeMorat, M. "Multiple Perceptions of Children's Aggression: Differences Across Neighborhood, Age, Gender, and Perceiver." *Psychology in the Schools,* 2001, *38,* 45–56.

Johnson, S., and Bolstad, O. "Methodological Issues in Naturalistic Observation: Some Problems and Solutions for Field Research." In L. Hamerlynch, J. Handy, and E. Mash (eds.), *Behavior Change: Methodology, Concepts, and Practice.* Champaign, Ill.: Research Press, 1973.

Lagerspetz, K., Bjorkqvist, K., and Peltonen, P. "Is Indirect Aggression Typical of Females? Gender Differences in Aggressiveness in 11 to 12 Year Old Children." *Aggressive Behavior,* 1988, *14,* 403–414.

Marsh, E., and Hedley, J. "Effect of Observer as a Function of Prior History of Social Interaction." *Perceptual and Motor Skills,* 1975, *40,* 659–669.

Martin, M., Gelfand, D., and Hartmann, D. "Effects of Adult and Peer Observers on Boys' and Girls' Responses to an Aggressive Model." *Child Development,* 1971, *41,* 1271–1275.

McMahon, R., and Frick, P. "Evidence-Based Assessment of Conduct Problems in Children and Adolescents." *Journal of Clinical Child and Adolescent Psychology,* 2005, *34,* 477–505.

Merrell, K. *Behavioral, Social, and Emotional Assessment of Children and Adolescents.* New York: Erlbaum, 2003.

Patterson, G., and Forgatch, M. "Predicting Future Clinical Adjustment from Treatment Outcome and Process Variables." *Psychological Assessment,* 1995, *7,* 275–285.

Pepler, D., and Craig, W. "A Peek Behind the Fence: Naturalistic Observations of Aggressive Children with Remote Audiovisual Recording." *Developmental Psychology,* 1995, *31,* 548–553.

Sluckin, A. *Growing Up in the Playground.* London: Routledge, 1981.

Smith, G., and Sheaffer, B. "Observer Reactivity in Monitored and Unmonitored Analogue Conditions." *Journal of Psychoeducational Assessment,* 1984, *2,* 249–255.

Thomas, D. *Some New Techniques for Studying Social Behavior.* New York: Columbia University Press, 1929.

CYNTHIA HUDLEY is professor in the Gevirtz Graduate School of Education at the University of California, Santa Barbara, and director of the graduate emphasis in Child and Adolescent Development.

7

This final chapter analyzes the content of the preceding examples, suggesting implications for the field of prevention research and practice.

Commentary on the Pitfalls and Pratfalls of Evaluation Research with Intervention and Prevention Programs

Karen L. Bierman

Although the concept of prevention as a strategy for reducing violence and related social problems is long standing, prevention science is a relatively new field of formal research inquiry. For example, the Center for Prevention Research at the National Institute of Health was first established in 1982; the Society for Prevention Research was incorporated in 1991. During the past two decades, initial prevention science efforts have focused heavily on defining standards for the identification of "best practices" in prevention and constructing catalogs of "proven programs" (for example, programs with documented impact in the context of rigorous, randomized controlled trials) (Kazdin and Weisz, 1998; Mihalic and others, 2004). These efforts have played a critical role in setting standards and improving access to high-quality violence prevention programs for dissemination in school- and community-based settings. At the same time, maximizing progress in prevention science requires a broad research agenda that moves beyond cataloguing past success. Ideally, the field can learn from each generation of prevention studies, increasing an understanding of change mechanisms that underlie successful violence prevention and systematically improving program impact in future trials.

The chapters in this volume demonstrate that, in addition to an approach focusing on positive findings, careful analyses of null or negative findings can also generate hypotheses concerning change mechanisms and impediments

NEW DIRECTIONS FOR EVALUATION, no. 110, Summer 2006 © Wiley Periodicals, Inc.
Published online in Wiley InterScience (www.interscience.wiley.com) • DOI: 10.1002/ev.189

to change, thereby guiding future program design. These chapters are important for two reasons: (1) they identify specific factors that can undermine prevention effectiveness in "real world" applications, and (2) they suggest methodological innovations that might be incorporated into future prevention research trials to better "postmortem" what went wrong when null or negative findings emerge and to suggest changes to improve future impact.

Flawed Model, Technology, or Execution?

These chapters illustrate that interventions may fail due to problems in any of three main areas. First, each intervention is based on a theoretical model that represents a formulation of risk and protective factors and a set of hypotheses linking proximal skills or contextual changes (targeted by the program) to reductions in distal risk (youth violence). Ideally, these theoretical models include hypotheses about mediation (the mechanisms and processes by which change in cognitions, behaviors, or contexts contributes causally to reductions in later risk) and about moderation (recognizing participant characteristics, such as developmental level, gender, or culture that may alter the effectiveness of the intervention). One reason an intervention may fail is that the theoretical model underlying the intervention is flawed. For example, in the PREP program (Parker, Asencio, and Plechner, 2006), the developers hypothesized that improved preplacement conditions and careful assessments would improve youth readiness for placement, thereby reducing preplacement time and improving placement outcomes. However, contrary to these hypotheses, the comfortable support of the PREP program appeared to encourage youth to stay in the program longer and to return to the program after placement, indicating a flaw in the causal model that provided a foundation for intervention design. A second example involves the moderation of intervention impact revealed in the analyses of the Metropolitan Area Child Study (MACS) (Guerra, Boxer, and Cook, 2006), in which the theoretical model of change guiding the intervention appeared accurate for the younger elementary children at the highest levels of risk, but served as an inadequate guide for interventions targeting the older preadolescent youth and the broader population of youth attending low-resource schools. In this latter case, part of the theoretical model might be maintained, but an expanded and differentiated model is needed to characterize alternative risk or protective mechanisms and diverging developmental trajectories characterizing youth at different developmental periods in varying ecological contexts.

In a different kind of problem scenario, the theoretical model underlying the intervention may be accurate, but the intervention may fail due to a problem in the technology of change, in that the intervention does not change the targeted proximal skills or contexts. For example, in the Youth Handgun Violence Prevention Project (YHVPP) (Williams and Mattson, 2006), the authors identified factors associated empirically with youth attitudes and behaviors regarding handguns and designed an intervention to modify those factors (for example, knowledge of the legal consequences of carrying and using handguns, attitudes reflecting excitement and power associated with handguns, and intentions to carry and use handguns). The authors postulated that intervention would induce changes in those attitudes and behaviors and thereby reduce violence. However, the intervention did not increase anti-handgun attitudes, knowledge of legal consequences, or youth intentions to carry handguns. In this case, the theoretical model underlying the intervention might have been correct (for example, that knowledge acquisition and attitude change may reduce handgun use), but changes in the intervention strategies themselves appear necessary to induce substantial changes in those knowledge and attitudinal mediators of violence reduction.

The Coping Power Program (Lochman and others, 2006) provides a particularly clear example of reduced intervention effectiveness associated with inadequate capacity to change certain attitudes and behaviors, specifically, parental decisions to engage in the intervention. Using propensity score analyses, these authors were able to document a positive impact on youth behavior change when parents engaged in intervention, supporting the theoretical model and effectiveness of the therapeutic change technologies used in the intervention program. Comparing those findings with results based on the total sample (intent to treat analyses), the authors also demonstrated that the relatively low level of overall parental involvement led to reduced (nonsignificant) program impact in the full population targeted. The comparison across analytic methods is instructive as it suggests a very specific area for future Coping Power Program innovation, namely strategies to improve parental recruitment and participation.

Sometimes, the source of the problem is less clear. For example, in the "See It and Stop It" media campaign to reduce dating violence (Rothman, Decker, and Silverman, 2006), ninth-grade youth who saw the advertisements did not visit the Web site for more information, resulting in low levels of exposure to the active intervention components. In this case, it is not clear whether the key problem was technological (for example, stronger change strategies were needed to compel youth to pursue the education offered at the Web site) or whether the theoretical model was flawed (for example, if they had pursued the education, would this have driven the social diffusion of behaviors and reduced dating violence, as proposed?). Nonetheless, understanding that exposure to the active intervention components was limited in this project can fuel innovative thinking to overcome this problem in a subsequent trial.

In general, distinguishing flaws in the underlying theoretical model informing the design of the intervention (which guides the selection of skills, behaviors, and attitudes for change) from weaknesses in the technology being used to change those targeted skills, attitudes, and behaviors is valuable. In the former case, the solution must be to rework the basic foundation of intervention design and rethink the intervention focus, whereas in the latter case, the target goals of the program may remain the same, but the technology brought to bear on inducing change must be strengthened.

A third, distinct problem affecting intervention impact involves the execution and fidelity of intervention implementation. Several of the studies described here faced major challenges during the implementation phase, particularly when the projects used service agency staff (rather than research project staff) for intervention delivery and evaluation data collection. For example, the YHVPP worked collaboratively with three human service agencies. Staff turnover and variations in staff understanding of and compliance with assessment and intervention protocols were challenges for this project, reducing the overall fidelity of implementation. Similarly, the PREP program found that high workloads and turnover decreased staff investment in and compliance with the intervention and research design. For prevention programs to have broad impact on the population, their widespread dissemination and community-based sustainability is critical. Hence, understanding how to improve staff engagement and fidelity of program implementation in "real-world" service settings represents a major challenge for prevention researchers (Greenberg, Domitrovich, and Bumbarger, 2001). Clearly, effective interventions require more than a good intervention program; program success in areas of provider engagement, staff training and professional development, and capacity to monitor and support high-fidelity implementation also affect program impact.

In summary, flaws in theory, flaws in the technology of change, and flaws in implementation execution can each cause an intervention to fail. Designing preventive intervention trials with data collection that fosters a differentiated understanding of those sources of potential intervention failure may enhance our capacity to learn from and improve ineffective interventions. Specific implications for future prevention research program design include (1) developing interventions with theoretical constructs in mind and measuring postulated moderating and mediating variables during the intervention trial in order to identify the location of program effects and to test the hypothetical model guiding the intervention, (2) including measures of participation and factors that may influence engagement to allow for propensity-score dose-response assessments as well as intent-to-treat analyses, and (3) assessing intervention implementation and fidelity. In addition, these papers underscore the importance of attending more carefully to the specific issues that challenge the impact of prevention programs as they move from well-controlled research settings into "real-world" implementation in practice settings.

Moving from Efficacy to Effectiveness

The Institute of Medicine (1994) describes a proscribed cycle for the development of preventive interventions. First, intervention programs are designed based on empirical research and developmental theory that identify risk and protective factors, as well as potentially effective intervention strategies. Then these interventions are tested in carefully controlled pilot studies to demonstrate program impact and efficacy. Finally, effective programs are transferred to the field and tested under "real-world" conditions, with implementation conducted by community-based service agencies. In this cycle, "efficacy" trials are distinguished from "effectiveness" trials. Whereas efficacy trials document that an intervention has beneficial effects when delivered under controlled conditions, with sample selection, intervention delivery, and assessment managed by the investigative team, effectiveness trials provide evidence that interventions have beneficial effects when delivered to heterogeneous samples in community-based settings by existing service agency staff (Weisz and Jensen, 1999). The ability to demonstrate impact is more difficult in effectiveness than efficacy trials, as program impact is affected by conditions such as implementation fidelity, measurement, portability and sustainability across contexts, and generalizability across a more heterogeneous set of participants. Prevention researchers are beginning to recognize the wide gap that exists between efficacy and effectiveness trials and the corresponding research issues that need to be addressed to improve the impact of effective interventions when implemented in "real world" settings (Glasgow, Lichtenstein, and Marcus, 2003).

One tension that must be addressed in moving from efficacy to effectiveness involves the relative value of research-based fidelity versus input and program adaptations offered by community members and local service providers. Ideally, prevention programs are able to balance this tension, using "real world" service delivery systems that are committed to implementing empirically proven prevention programs with high fidelity to the efficacy protocols, while also providing the active involvement and input so critical to assuring that the program is locally and culturally relevant and designed in a way that lends itself to practical implementation within the community and service context (Biglan, Mrazek, Carnine, and Flay, 2003). Moving from efficacy to effectiveness thus requires attention to local, cultural, and context-relevant adaptations based upon the input of school and community partners; yet, adaptations that are too extensive or involve changes in the core intervention model or change strategies run the risk of decreasing fidelity and thereby decreasing impact.

Relevant to this tension, Weissberg and Greenberg (1998) have contrasted the assumptions underlying the relatively new prevention science model and the more long-standing collaborative community action research model. In the former, program designs are based primarily upon research documenting the risk and protective factors associated with targeted mental health problems, combined with randomized-controlled efficacy trials that document the positive impact of specific intervention strategies on those outcomes. In this model, the dissemination challenge is to move the empirically validated procedures into the field. In contrast, the collaborative community action research model is based on an ecological perspective that emphasizes the critical involvement of community members in partnership with researchers in all phases of program development and design, assuming that effective program design requires local wisdom and engagement for success. A danger associated with collaborative models of prevention program design is that community and school-based coalitions may make decisions about intervention programming based upon consensus or local wisdom, in some cases with little regard for existing developmental and clinical research. Weissberg and Greenberg (1998) argue compellingly for the need to combine the strengths of these two approaches, developing program design and delivery strategies that involve community leaders and participants in all phases of decision making, but that also make maximal use of available research regarding developmental patterns, risk and protective factors, and empirically proven intervention strategies (see also the Conduct Problems Prevention Research Group [CPPRG], 2002). Correspondingly, an integrated approach challenges prevention researchers to do a better job of providing school and community partners with the technical assistance, information, and professional development opportunities that allow them to take greater advantage of the empirical literature when thinking about local service needs and programming.

In addition, several of the studies presented in this volume highlight the need for greater attention to factors that affect the likely adoption, integration, and sustained maintenance of interventions over time by local service agencies. In several studies, including MACS, YHVPP, and PREP, researchers described how staff turnover, heavy work loads and competing work demands, and limited training and supervision affected the commitment and capacity of teachers, group leaders, referral agencies, and other service providers to support the preventive interventions. In some cases (PREP), changes in the political and economic climate affected the policies and financing for the program, resulting in premature termination. Certainly, the challenges of creating sustainable programs that can be integrated into existing service delivery systems are different from those involved in initiating programs, particularly when the goal is to maintain the program in a way that sustains high levels of fidelity over time. The research base in this area is just beginning to accumulate. For example, examining the Communities That Care program (Hawkins and Catalano, 1992), which uses community coalitions to select and monitor prevention programming, Greenberg, Feinberg, Gomez, and Osgood (2005) identified several critical factors that affected program sustainability: (1) the expertise of individuals in key leadership positions, particularly their knowledge and understanding of empirically-based prevention programs, (2) the quality of initial program fidelity and implementation, (3) characteristics of the service delivery system, including both the internal functioning and effectiveness of the school-community CTC coalition and the support and commitment to the program by school leaders, particularly principals and staff involved in delivery (Kam, Greenberg, and Walls, 2003; Paine-Andrews and others,

2000), and (4) the availability of sustained funding (Marek, Mancini, and Brock, 2000).

To begin to close the gap between efficacy and effectiveness research, more careful consideration and research is needed on those factors that influence the processes of community adoption, implementation, and sustainability as these factors appear critical to long-term program impact. Specific suggestions for future research in the area of youth violence prevention include a continued commitment to the use of developmental and epidemiological research and rigorous, randomized-controlled trials as a basis for program development and design. Emerging across studies, for example, violence prevention programs appear more effective when they are based upon sound theoretical rationales, address developmentally proven risk and protective factors, use cognitive or behavioral strategies to improve competencies and skills associated with self-regulation, and address family, school, and neighborhood factors associated with youth adaptation. At the same time, greater attention to field implementation and sustainability at the outset of prevention program design is also needed. Suggestions include: (1) involving the target audience and program providers in formative assessments and intervention and evaluation design from the beginning in order to enhance local fit and commitment; (2) designing interventions with a consideration of the field-based challenges, including attention to the ease with which implementation can be accomplished; (3) attending carefully to the quality of the training materials, designing them for a range of potential providers who may vary in educational background and prior experience; (4) providing clearly articulated implementation protocols; and (5) supporting ongoing supervision and professional development opportunities, with accountability to program fidelity at both the provider and supervisor level. In addition, continued research into the factors influencing participant engagement, implementation fidelity, and program sustainability is needed to guide future program design.

Additional Issues in Prevention Research Design and Methodology

In addition to the issues described above, the papers in this volume also illustrate the challenges that prevention research methodology faces in the field. Participant recruitment and engagement continue to be major challenges in most areas of prevention programming. Unlike treatment studies that are focused on serving participants who are seeking help in clinic settings, prevention programs typically target a broader segment of the population, either the entire population (as in universal prevention programs) or individuals at elevated risk for the problem outcomes (as in selective or indicated prevention programs). In either case, prevention programs seek to intervene prior to the emergence of significant disorder, but therefore face particular challenges in engaging their target populations, who may have little awareness of their risk and reduced motivation to seek help.

Measurement and the assessment of meaningful change is another critical challenge for prevention research. This challenge was most clearly illustrated by the BrainPower program (Hudley, 2006), in which the use of behavioral observations (well validated in research studies) proved difficult and less valid when translated into the field and implemented by a range of school personnel. In addition, several projects struggled with the process of tracking participants in the field for post-intervention and follow-up assessment. At least one project (See It and Stop It) also suffered from competing interventions being implemented with the control comparison group, and several projects raised the question of whether the time frame of the research design was sufficient to allow prevention effects to emerge. These methodological challenges are not unique to effectiveness trials, but are more likely to pose unique difficulties for researchers as the control over trial and evaluation implementation moves into community settings and community providers. The papers in this volume illustrate the challenge and provide a "heads up" for future researchers concerning design issues that warrant careful consideration.

Conclusions and Future Directions

Prevention science is moving from a narrow emphasis on cataloging success to a broader research agenda that takes aim at the difficult gap between research-based efficacy and community-based effectiveness. This volume, which gathers "lessons learned" from youth violence prevention programs that failed to produce significant results in community settings, illustrates the difficulty of the challenge and highlights the value of careful reflection on past efforts to improve future designs. Moving beyond the initial demonstration of effective programs, future research must identify characteristics of delivery systems that can provide broad access to locally and culturally relevant, high fidelity, empirically supported youth violence prevention programs over sustained periods of time. Further prevention research is needed, using trials in a multifaceted way: (1) to test elaborated theoretical models (examining mediation and moderation by individual and contextual characteristics), (2) to strengthen therapeutic technologies that elicit improved engagement and induce greater attitude and behavior change, and (3) to improve the quality of implementation fidelity and sustained portability in community service settings. At the end of the day, proven programs will be those that produce statistically and clinically significant findings in the context of rigorous, community-based, randomized-controlled designs. Along the way, however, designing preventive interventions to support more complete and effective post-mortem analyses may increase the value demonstrated in this volume of interventions that held promise, but lacked the level of impact desired. It is difficult but critically important work, with the potential to dramatically reduce youth violence and improve youth well-being and societal success.

References

Biglan, A., Mrazek, P. J., Carnine, D., and Flay, B. R. "The Integration of Research and Practice in the Prevention of Youth Problem Behaviors." *American Psychologist*, 2003, *58*, 433–440.

Conduct Problems Prevention Research Group. "The Implementation of the Fast Track Program: An Example of a Large-Scale Prevention Science Efficacy Trial." *Journal of Abnormal Child Psychology*, 2002, *30*, 1–17.

Glasgow, R. E., Lichtenstein, E., and Marcus, A. "Why Don't We See More Translation of Health Promotion Research to Practice? Rethinking the Efficacy to Effectiveness Transition." *American Journal of Public Health*, 2003, *93*, 1261–1267.

Greenberg, M. T., Feinberg, M., Gomez, B., and, Osgood, D W. "Testing a Community Prevention Focused Model of Coalition Functioning and Sustainability: A Comprehensive Study of Communities That Care in Pennsylvania." In T. Stockwell, P. Gruenewald, J. Toumbourou, and W. Loxley (eds), *Preventing Harmful Substance Use: The Evidence Base for Policy and Practice*. New York: Wiley, 2005.

Greenberg, M. T., Domitrovich, C., and Bumbarger, B. "The Prevention of Mental Disorders in School-Aged Children: Current State of the Field." *Prevention and Treatment*, 2001, *4*, Article 1. Retrieved March 1, 2002, from http://journals.apa.org/prevention/volume4/pre0040001a.html.

Guerra, N. G., Boxer, P., and Cook, C. R. "What Works (and What Does Not) in Youth Violence Prevention: Rethinking the Questions and Finding New Answers." In R. N. Parker and C. Hudley (eds.), *Pitfalls and Pratfalls: Issues of Null and Negative Findings in Evaluating Interventions*. New Directions for Evaluation, no. 110. San Francisco: Jossey-Bass, 2006.

Hawkins, J. D., and Catalano, R. F., Jr. *Communities That Care: Action for Drug Abuse Prevention*. San Francisco, Calif.: Jossey-Bass, 1992.

Hudley, C. "Who Is Watching the Watchers? Observing Peer Interactions on Elementary School Playgrounds." In R. N. Parker and C. Hudley (eds.), *Pitfalls and Pratfalls: Issues of Null and Negative Findings in Evaluating Interventions*. New Directions for Evaluation, no. 110. San Francisco: Jossey-Bass, 2006.

Institute of Medicine. *Reducing Risks for Mental Disorders: Frontiers for Preventive Intervention Research*. Washington, D.C.: National Academy Press, 1994.

Kam, C. M., Greenberg, M. T., and Wells, C. "Examining the Role of Implementation Quality in School-Based Prevention Using the PATHS Curriculum." *Prevention Science*, 2003, *4*, 55–63.

Kazdin, A. E., and Weisz, J. R. "Identifying and Developing Empirically Supported Child and Adolescent Treatments." *Journal of Consulting and Clinical Psychology*, 1998, *66*, 19–36.

Lochman, J. E., Boxmayer, C., Powell, N., Roth, D. L., and Windle, M. "Masked Intervention Effects: Implications of Low Dosage of Intervention on Outcomes." In R. N. Parker and C. Hudley (eds.), *Pitfalls and Pratfalls: Issues of Null and Negative Findings in Evaluating Interventions*. New Directions for Evaluation, no. 110. San Francisco: Jossey-Bass, 2006.

Marek, L. I., Mancini, J. A., and Brock, D.J. *The National Youth at Risk Program Sustainability Study*. Report to the USDA, Washington, D.C., 2000.

Mihalic, S., Fagan, A. A., Irwin, K., Ballard, D., and Elliott, D. *Blueprints for Violence Prevention*. Washington, D.C.: Office of Juvenile Justice and Delinquency Prevention, 2004.

Paine-Andrews, A., Fisher, J., Campuzano, M. K., Fawcett, S. B., and Berkly-Patton, J. "Promoting Sustainability of Community Health Initiatives: An Empirical Case Study." *Health Promotion Practice*, 2000, *1*, 248–258.

Parker, R. N., Asencio, E. K., and Plechner, D. "How Much of a Good Thing Is Too Much? Explaining the Failure of a Well-Designed, Well-Executed Intervention in Juvenile Hall for 'Hard-to-Place' Delinquents." In R. N. Parker and C. Hudley (eds.), *Pitfalls and Pratfalls: Issues of Null and Negative Findings in Evaluating Interventions.* New Directions for Evaluation, no. 110. San Francisco: Jossey-Bass, 2006.

Rothman, E. F., Decker, M. R., and Silverman, J. G. "Evaluation of a Teen Dating Violence Social Marketing Campaign: Lessons Learned and Future Directions." In R. N. Parker and C. Hudley (eds.), *Pitfalls and Pratfalls: Issues of Null and Negative Findings in Evaluating Interventions.* New Directions for Evaluation, no. 110. San Francisco: Jossey-Bass, 2006.

Weissberg, R. P., and Greenberg, M. T. "School and Community Competence-Enhancement and Prevention Programs." In I. E. Siegel and K. A. Renninger (eds.), *Handbook of Child Psychology. Vol. 4: Child Psychology in Practice* (5th ed.). New York: Wiley, 1998, 877–954.

Weisz, J., and Jensen, P. "Efficacy and Effectiveness of Child and Adolescent Psychotherapy and Pharmacotherapy." *Mental Health Services Research,* 1999, *1*(3), 125–157.

Williams, K. R., and Mattson, S. A. "Qualitative Lessons from a Community-Based Violence Prevention Project with Null Findings." In R. N. Parker and C. Hudley (eds.), *Pitfalls and Pratfalls: Issues of Null and Negative Findings in Evaluating Interventions.* New Directions for Evaluation, no. 110. San Francisco: Jossey-Bass, 2006.

KAREN L. BIERMAN *is director of the Children, Youth, and Families Consortium at the Pennsylvania State University, where she is also Distinguished Professor of Clinical Child Psychology.*

INDEX

Back Issue/Subscription Order Form

Back Issues: Please send me the following issues at $27 each
(Important: please include series initials and issue number, such as EV101.)

_____

_____

_____

$ _____ Total for single issues

$ _____ Shipping charges:

	Surface	Domestic	Canadian
First item		$5.00	$6.00
Each add'l item		$3.00	$1.50

For next-day and second-day delivery rates, call the number listed above.

Subscriptions: Please ___ start ___ renew my subscription to *New Directions for Evaluation* for the year 2_____ at the following rate:

U.S.	___ Individual $80	___ Institutional $185
Canada	___ Individual $80	___ Institutional $225
All others	___ Individual $104	___ Institutional $259

Online subscriptions are available via Wiley InterScience!

**For more information about online subscriptions visit
www.wileyinterscience.com**

$_____ Total single issues and subscriptions (Add appropriate sales tax for your state for single issue orders. No sales tax for U.S. subscriptions. Canadian residents, add GST for subscriptions and single issues.)

___ Payment enclosed (U.S. check or money order only)

___ VISA ___ MC ___ AmEx # _____ Exp. date _____

Signature _____ Day Phone _____

___ Bill me (U.S. institutional orders only. Purchase order required.)

Purchase order # _____

Federal Tax ID13559302   GST 89102 8052

Name _____

Address _____

_____

Phone _____ E-mail _____

For more information about Jossey-Bass, visit our Web site at www.josseybass.com

NEW DIRECTIONS FOR EVALUATION
IS NOW AVAILABLE ONLINE AT WILEY INTERSCIENCE

What is Wiley InterScience?

Wiley InterScience is the dynamic online content service from John Wiley & Sons delivering the full text of over 300 leading scientific, technical, medical, and professional journals, plus major reference works, the acclaimed Current Protocols laboratory manuals, and even the full text of select Wiley print books online.

What are some special features of Wiley InterScience?

Wiley Interscience Alerts is a service that delivers table of contents via e-mail for any journal available on Wiley InterScience as soon as a new issue is published online.
Early View is Wiley's exclusive service presenting individual articles online as soon as they are ready, even before the release of the compiled print issue. These articles are complete, peer-reviewed, and citable.
CrossRef is the innovative multi-publisher reference linking system enabling readers to move seamlessly from a reference in a journal article to the cited publication, typically located on a different server and published by a different publisher.

How can I access Wiley InterScience?

Visit http://www.interscience.wiley.com.

Guest Users can browse Wiley InterScience for unrestricted access to journal Tables of Contents and Article Abstracts, or use the powerful search engine.
Registered Users are provided with a *Personal Home Page* to store and manage customized alerts, searches, and links to favorite journals and articles. Additionally, Registered Users can view free Online Sample Issues and preview selected material from major reference works.
Licensed Customers are entitled to access full-text journal articles in PDF, with select journals also offering full-text HTML.

How do I become an Authorized User?

Authorized Users are individuals authorized by a paying Customer to have access to the journals in Wiley InterScience. For example, a University that subscribes to Wiley journals is considered to be the Customer.
Faculty, staff and students authorized by the University to have access to those journals in Wiley InterScience are Authorized Users. Users should contact their Library for information on which Wiley journals they have access to in Wiley InterScience.

DATE DUE

GAYLORD | PRINTED IN U.S.A.